Chinese Martial Arts Series 1
T'ai Chi Ch'uan
The Basic Exercises

Chinese Martial Arts Series 1

T'ai Chi Ch'uan
The Basic Exercises

Technical Supervisor,
Professor Wang Peikuen

Written and performed by
Xing Yanling
(Shing Yenling)

Translated into English by
Mei Xuexiong
(Mei Sueshiong)

SUGAWARA MARTIAL ARTS / JAPAN PUBLICATIONS

Chinese Martial Arts Series 1
T'ai Chi Ch'uan—The Basic Exercises
ISBN:0-87040-849-6
Written and Performed by Xing Yanling
Under the technical supervision of Professor Wang Peikun
Translated into English from Chinese by Mei Xuexiong
Photographed by Sadao Hirata, Apollo Soken Co., Ltd.
Edited by Tetsutaka Sugawara, Xing Yanling

Published by

SUGAWARA MARTIAL ARTS INSTITUTE, INC.
20-13, Tadao 3 chome, Machida-shi, Tokyo, 194 Japan.
Phone: 0427-94-0972 Fax: 0427-94-0899
E-mail: TSugawar@ga2.so-net.or.jp

First printing: March 1990
Sixth printing: June 1997
Printed in Japan

Distributors:
United States: Kodansha America, Inc. through Oxford University Press, 198 Madison Avenue, New York, NY 10016. *Canada:* Fitzhenry & Whiteside Ltd., 195 Allstate Parkway, Markham, Ontario L3R 4T8. *United Kingdom and Europe:* Premier Book Marketing Ltd., 1 Gower Street, London WC1E 6HA. *Australia and New Zealand:* Bookwise International, 54 Crittenden Road, Findon, South Australia 5023. *The Far East and Japan:* Japan Publications Trading Co., Ltd., 1-2-1, Sarugaku-cho, Chiyoda-ku, Tokyo 101, Japan.

Simplified Twenty-Four Movements Taijiquan

Forty-Eight Movements Taijiquan

Preface

T'ai Chi Ch'uan (taijiquan) — **The Basic Exercises**, one of the Chinese martial arts series, is now in published form. I am sure that it will be well received by both domestic and foreign practitioners.

Taijiquan is one of the main branches of Chinese martial arts. It not only has an extensive mass foundation in China, but has spread far and wide among people in many other countries in recent years. Taijiquan enthusiasts from all over the world either come to China to study, regardless of the trouble of travelling a long distance, or learn under the direction of Chinese experts invited to give lessons abroad. More and more people are interested in taijiquan, and even those who have learnt it from Chinese experts and have got some understanding of their own have joined the ranks to spread and popularize it. Taijiquan, a valuable traditional Chinese exercise, will certainly be widely spread and bring benefit to mankind.

A deeper understanding of taijiquan's health-building and restorative effects is now available. Through exercising themselves in taijiquan, sedentary people can build up their level of fitness, and patients suffering from chronic diseases can improve their physical health and thus extricate themselves from long-term suffering. Taijiquan can also be of benefit to the restoration of health after patients are cured of their illnesses. In addition, taijiquan is conducive to self-cultivation, as well as strong physique because by regular practice, practitioners can mold their temperament and foster positive personal qualities such as calmness, sobriety, restraint of impetuosity and anger. When their training has reached a high enough degree of skill, they can also begin to develop skills in attack and defense for the purpose of self-protection.

Shing Yen-Ling, the authoress of this book, graduated from the Physical Education Department of Fukien Teachers' University, majoring in Chinese martial arts. After graduation, she entered the Wuhan Institute of

Physical Culture for further training. Often, during national martial arts tournaments and exhibitions, she managed to obtain advice from famous old professors or experts, and she studied assiduously. While working in Fukien Institute of Traditional Chinese medicine, as a head coach, she specialized in teaching Chinese martial arts and training the institute team members. She is also a first-grade martial arts judge. For more than ten years she has engaged in the theoretical and technical research on taijiquan, Eight-diagram Palm, Long Shadow Boxing, both with bare hands and with weapons, and has achieved great success in this field.

What needs to be particularly pointed out is that she is always good at teaching students in accordance with their aptitude. It is due to her superb ability to arrange course content, to plan the course schedule, and to select the adequate teaching methods, all according to the different dispositions, interests, physical conditions and achievement levels of the students, that she has been highly praised by practitioners both in China and abroad.

This series is a summation of her teaching experience in Taijiquan, Taiji-swordplay and Eight-diagram Palm. In this book, the writer introduces the elementary sets of taijiquan by means of clear photograph sequences and succinct explanations of the movements, making it easier for the readers to learn by imitation. In simple words, she also summarizes the features, functions and basic rules of taijiquan as well as the way to practice, so that practitioners can make constant improvement under the guidance of this book. It is clearly a good reference manual for both beginners and self-taught practitioners of taijiquan.

The writer and the publisher have asked me to write a few words to this book and I am glad to do so. I am quite sure that their great efforts to spread and develop taijiquan in the form of their books will bring fitness and happiness to people all over the world.

Wang Peikuen
Shanghai Institute of Physical Education
August 25, 1989

Acknowledgments

This is the first volume of the Chinese martial arts series. I am lucky to have a good chance to introduce my favorite sports, which I have enjoyed for many years. I would like to thank my many teachers and colleagues for their enthusiastic help, particularly Professor Guo Ming-Hua, Hu Jin-Huan, Physical Education Department, Fukien Teachers' University, the late Professor Wen Jing-Ming, Liu Yu-Hua, Mr. Zhang Hong-Chao, Mr. Zhang Ke-Jian, Wuhan Institute of Physical Culture, Madame Kan Gui-Xiang, Beijing Institute of P.E., who has taught and guided me for the past thirteen years. Thanks are especially due to Mr. Wang Peikun, Professor of Shanghai Institute of Physical Culture and Vice-Chairman of the Shanghai Martial Arts Association, who, in the midst of his pressing affairs, contributed greatly to the revision of this book and also wrote the preface.

I wish to express my heartfelt thanks to Mr. Mei Xue-Xiong, P.E. Department, Fukien Teachers' University, for his permission to translate this book.

I am deeply indebted to Mr. Sugawara Tetsutaka, Minato Research and Publishing Company and Sugawara Martial Arts Institute, Japan, who has offered great energies to the publication of this Chinese martial arts series. Many thanks are also due to the Japan Publications Trading Company and Mr. Meik Skoss, Secretary of the Japan Martial Arts Society, for his pertinent proofreading for this volume.

I hope everyone will like this book, the success of which results from wide cooperation.

Xing Yanling
(Shing Yenling)

February, 1990

CONTENTS

Introduction

Taijiquan (t'ai chi ch'uan) is one of the principal branches of the Chinese martial arts (wushu). It has been known for a long time. In recent years, a wushu craze has come into being with the rapid popularization of Chinese martial arts. As a result of this great fervor, the health-building and restorative values of taijiquan have been recognized all over the world. At present, not only Chinese martial arts teachers, but many people from other countries who are interested in the extension of martial arts are teaching people how to practice taijiquan. As more and more people learn taijiquan, its international influence is becoming increasingly great. The exchange of taijiquan is no longer confined to ordinary people. Open competition has existed for some time. In March, 1989, when the Second Dual Meet of Taijiquan between China and Japan took place in Shanghai, China, there were not only 80 masters competing in the arena, but 200 participants from each side exhibiting as well. The excitement and the novelty of sight were of great magnificence. In 1990, in the Eleventh Asian Games in Beijing, Wushu will appear as one of the formal events, among which will be taijiquan.

The martial arts are part of traditional Chinese culture and have also had a close relationship with Chinese medicine, throughout their history; taijiquan, as one of the martial arts, has thus been very well received by people interested in Chinese medicine as well as enthusiasts in personal fitness. It is also a required course for students of Chinese medicine. I have given taijiquan lessons in an institute of traditional Chinese medicine for years and have had some understanding of my own.

Thanks to the efforts of many years, the popularization and the raising of taijiquan standards have achieved remarkable success, but I still want to do what little I can in order to spread Chinese martial arts better, so that this cultural heritage can be shared with people all over the world. So I have made so bold as to sum up my practice and teaching experience, both in China and abroad, and introduce them to people interested in Chinese martial arts through pictures and brief explanations.

In order to suit the needs of practitioners of different ages, physical condition or interests, the relatively easy and uncomplicated Simplified 24 Movements Taijiquan, 48 Movements Taijiquan, Chen Style Simplified Taijiquan, Taiji-swordplay and Eight-diagram Palm have been selected for presentation in a series of books on Chinese martial arts. May every practitioner be sound in mind and body, and live a long life.

1. The Characteristics of Taijiquan

1) Since taijiquan is part of the Chinese martial arts, a type of traditional exercise, it belongs to the realm of physical culture and has some features of sport. Exercising in taijiquan is obviously a good way to build up one's health. It has also been proved that taijiquan possesses certain curative and restorative powers and that is one of the reasons why it has become so popular with men and women, young and old alike, in recent years.

2) Most actions in the Chinese martial arts have implications of attack and defense. Without exception, the movements in taijiquan are composed of skills and techniques of striking, kicking, throwing and joint-locking. Although gentle and slow movements are usually required when practicing Yang, Wu, or Sun Style taijiquan, there is also the Chen Style. The major features of this style are a combination of vigor and gentleness, alternating between quickness and slowness. To analyze the meanings of attack-defense which are embodied in the movements can not only arouse practitioners' interests for learning, but will also contribute to the correct performance of the movements. One can first learn the use of attack-defense techniques in taijiquan and then proceed to grasp more practical skills for combat.

3) One outstanding feature of taijiquan is that it is usually described as "having both form and spirit", "combining inside and outside into one". As the movements of taijiquan are extracted from combative techniques, it is essential that movements should be performed in the spirit of attack-defense. On the other hand, all movements should be in harmony with one's breath and conscious thought, so that the unity of internal spirit and external appearance can be achieved. This feature is a characteristic attribute of Chinese martial arts, and it also reflects the traditional style of the Chinese nation. The distinctive features of Chinese martial arts can emerge only if one follows this pattern while practicing taijiquan, otherwise the movements will merely become a dance or general exercise.

4) Taijiquan has substantial content, with several schools such as Chen, Wu, Sun and Yang, and multitudinous simplified or newly-composed series based on the older styles. Its widespread adaptability allows it to satisfy the various demands of people of different ages or physical conditions, and to meet the needs of patients suffering from different illnesses. As regards the climate, training area, and clothing and equipmemt necessary, taijiquan is more convenient and easier to perform than other sports, because it requires almost nothing special for exercise. One can make do with whatever is available, anywhere, and that is one of the most practical advantages of taijiquan.

2. The Way To Practice Taijiquan

1) Tranquil Mind and Relaxed Body

"Tranquil mind" means that, while practicing taijiquan, the mind should be calm and not think of anything else. With consciousness commanding the movements, the attention must be concentrated on the details of every motion so that the implications of attack-defense can be manifested through the absorbed spirit, and the so-called state of "body goes where spirit reaches" can be achieved.

"Tranquil mind" can enhance excitability in motor-nerve centers, thereby contributing to the regulation of functions of the central nervous system and speeding up the removal of fatigue in other areas of the cerebral cortex. All of these will result in improvements of function of other bodily organs. "Tranquil mind" can also be conducive to integration of movements and the combination of internal spirit and external appearance, thereby improving the quality of exercise.

"Relaxed body" means that the postures should be natural and relaxed, all muscles, joints and ligaments should be comfortable, so that every part of the limbs and trunk can bend or extend freely and naturally. The key to this is that, with the whole body relaxed and with consciousness directing the breath and motion, all movements remain smooth and fluid, all muscles neither stiff nor rigid, but not flaccid or lacking in strength.

2) Continuous and Circular Movement

From start to finish, all the movements should be closely linked in an endless chain, without any obvious interruption or stopping. As described in an ancient essay on taijiquan, "they should follow one another continuously, like the smooth running water in a long river or in a wide ocean," with the end of one movement being the beginning of the next. Any break between movements will result in a sense of disharmony.

On the other hand, taijiquan distinguishes itself from other martial arts by its unique circular path of motion. Limbs always move in circles or curves, changing from one position to another freely, naturally, and smoothly. In order to follow this pattern, one should keep both the upper and lower limbs in a natural curve and avoid any direct impact or straight twist.

3) Gentleness and Evenness

Except for some vigorous actions, most movements of taijiquan should be carried out gently and evenly. Practitioners should keep at an unhurried and uniform pace throughout the exercise, avoiding going fast one moment and slow the next. There is a vivid expression in a taijiquan classic describing the application of strength which may be translated into English as "utilizing one's strength in the same way as reeling off raw silk from a cocoon." It is absolutely necessary to keep each part of the body in smooth and constant motion. But the practitioner must remember that slower is by no means the better. The pace should never be lowered to a point that any interruption appears.

4) Coordination of Upper and Lower Halves of the Body

Body movements should be well coordinated throughout the entire exercise. The upper limbs should move in cooperation with the lower ones and vice versa, whether the action is complex or simple. It is very important to use the waist as the main axis of movement in order to achieve perfect harmony. Whatever part is in motion, the rest should follow. It is often described so "a single movement sets the whole body moving", and this reveals the meaning of the word "coordination".

5) Concordance of Internal (Spirit) and External (Form)

In practicing taijiquan, the mind is dominant, guiding the practitioner's movements throughout the practice. Moreover, the breath should be well coordinated with the movements. In this respect, the awareness and breath are the inside and the body movements are the outside. Practitioners should focus their attention on physical actions and make their eyes follow the motions of the hands so that the internal awareness can be manifested through the bright expression of the eyes. It may be described as "eyes following the hands," or "eyes resting where the hand reaches". On the other hand, when practitioners get more skilled in body movements, they must be able to adjust their breath to the pace and the manner of motion so they can not only act smoothly and freely, but also breathe evenly and naturally. In particular, such actions as opening, stretching, extending, and rising are usually accompanied by inhaling; conversely, such actions as closing, bending, contracting, and falling are usually accompanied by exhaling. When spirit, breath and movement are in perfect harmony, the concordance of internal and external is no longer an elusive goal, but a manifested ability.

6) Clear Distinction Between Emptiness and Solidity

The "empty-solid" transformation is an outstanding feature of taijiquan. When an action is viewed as a whole, the completed posture is solid, while the process of motion is empty. When an action is analysed partially, the leg which bears most of the weight is solid, while the leg which moves or assists to support the body is empty; the limbs which express the main substance of the motion are solid, while the limbs which play merely a subsidiary role are empty. It requires substantial and steady movements to be solid, but unhindered and implicit ones to be empty.

Emptiness and solidness are relative and they change constantly from one to the other. With awareness of what should be empty and what should be solid, the practitioner must pay attention to the shift of his weight, the movements of his limbs and the distribution of his strength, so that he can not only distinguish between emptiness and solidness clearly, but also transform them naturally and flexibly. It is impossible for the practitioner to keep body and limbs well balanced if he fails in this basic rule.

3. Basic Body Positions

1) The Head

Keep the head erect, with the neck naturally relaxed and chin drawn slightly in. Coordinate movement of the neck with the change in position of the body and turning of the torso, but do not allow the head to sway. The facial expression should be natural. Breathe through the nose with the mouth closed naturally.

Correct form   **Bad form**

The head should be erect and look forward.

2) The Trunk

a) Chest and Back

One of the basic rules is "keeping the chest in and the back extended." This description means that the practitioner should not throw out his chest, should allow the muscles on his back to stretch freely as the arms are in motion, so that there can be a sense of "back up". In fact, the muscles on both the chest and the back should be relaxed to eliminate tension on the ribs. This ensures natural breathing. Be sure not to make the mistake of a hunched back.

b) Waist

The waist, namely the lumbar spine, is the mainstay of the body. As a pivotal point of movement, it plays a very important role in harmonizing movement, regulating posture, and balancing the body. While practicing, be sure to keep the waist relaxed and the spine naturally upright, so as to ensure freedom in turning and changes of position. Do not thrust out the belly or hunch the waist because that will impair flexibility and integration of movement.

c) Hips

Hold the hips slightly in and avoid protruding them out, so as not to spoil the natural posture. This, along with a relaxed waist, enables the practitioner not only to keep his body more stable but to move his legs more nimbly as well. The hips however, should not be tensed excessively as this may restrict the freedom of the waist or hinder the action of the legs.

Correct form   **Bad forms**

The upper body is a little slouch. The hip is not correct. ❷

The upper body bending backward. ❸

3) The Legs

Actions of the legs are of great importance to the stability and balance of the body and the flexibility and deftness in stepping. Therefore, in practice, special care must be given to the position of both feet, the bending of the legs, and the transformation between emptiness and solidness while shifting the weight.

In moving the legs, the crotch should be kept relaxed and the legs bent at the knees. The lifting and lowering of the feet should be light and deft. On stepping, one leg bears the weight to keep the body stable, the other leg moves slowly. When going forward, rest the heel first on the floor; when going backward, put the ball of the foot down before the entire foot is gradually set firm. When taking a step sideways, rest the toes on the floor first; then the sole and heel. The "toes-first" manner is also required for the follow-up step and the skip step. The rising and dropping of the thigh should be gentle and slow.

4) The Arms

The elementary rule for the arms is often termed "shoulders sunk and elbows dropped," meaning that the joints of these body parts should be relaxed and lowered. Do not shrug the shoulders during practice. When the arm extends, it never goes so far as to be completely straight, nor does it bend excessively. In fact, the arms should be well rounded throughout the whole sequence, avoiding any straight or angled movement.

The rule for the hands is "fingers extended out and wrists kept down." It requires the practitioner to stretch his fingers naturally, with the palms slightly cupped and the wrists a little dropped. The movements of the hands should be in line with those of arms. Much attention must be paid to the subtle changes of the hands which often result from the rotation of the arms.

The level of the right elbow is too high.

4. The Benefits of Taijiquan

1) Building up a good physique in a balanced manner.

Taijiquan does a lot of good for the skeleton, muscles and joints of the body. As mentioned above, since a single movement will set the whole body moving, all the muscles and joints will be in motion as long as the practitioner starts the exercise in the right way. Regular practice will no doubt result in an all-round and concordant development of physique, and this is one of the reasons why taijiquan has been so popular with people since ancient times.

2) Giving consideration to both inside and outside.

Not only are the movements of all muscles and joints good for fitness, but the highly concentrated attention; deep, sound breathing; and the concordance between consciousness, breath and movement can enormously improve the regulating functions of the central nervous system and thus benefit the whole body, especially the internal organs.

3) Molding the temperament.

Taijiquan movements are all linked in a continuous chain. They should be carried out gently and slowly. Therefore, it requires the practitioner be fully placid, and thus helps to cultivate restraint and contributes to the control of impulsive character. This can be good for people for getting along well with each other in such a complicated society as ours.

4) Curing illness and recovering health.

It is true that taijiquan possesses several favourable features that make it more and more popular with people, but its therapeutic effects are the main factor which makes people think highly of the art. It has been scientifically proved that taijiquan can produce certain influences upon each of the main systems of the human body, especially the central nervous system, the cardiovascular system, the respiratory system and the digestive system. Actually, taijiquan is beneficial to patients suffering from chronic diseases such as high blood pressure, stomach ulcers, heart trouble, arthritis and neurasthenia. Although the gentle and smooth movements of taijiquan do not consume much energy, the loads do vary with different duration, frequency and height of stance, which makes it possible for patients to take suitable exercise in accord with their physical condition.

5. Points for Attention

1) Do not be overanxious for rapid success.

Since the movements of taijiquan have complex external forms and profound substance, the practitioner should never be impatient for quick results. Otherwise, he will merely copy the actions mechanically and can not realize the essence of the art. In addition, if the trainee always demands more and seeks quick results, the movements inevitably can not be up to standard. Once he realizes the need for correction, it will be too difficult to do because of the motor habits already formed. It is often described as "easy to learn but difficult to correct." So, with the emphasis on quality, the beginner should not ask for too much at first. Proceed to the next form only after the previous movements can be executed quite accurately.

2) Learn forms first.

Forms mean the appearances of the movements. It is necessary that the beginner first learn the movements of taijiquan according to the name list of the movements. He should imitate the movements, as taught by the instructor, as closely as possible and bear them in mind. Through training, he will gradually manage to make his own movements similar in appearance to the standard ones of the instructor. Generally, beginners should first practice in a big form (with expansive movements) before they training in a small form, as described "seeking for expansion first, then compactness," because a big form is more conducive to better understanding and a better grasp of the movements.

While learning the forms, special care must be given to the position of every part of the body. The implications of attack-defense embodied in the movements should never be neglected in this stage.

3) Follow the correct order of movements and advance step by step.

In the process of learning the forms, the basic rules of taijiquan must be emphasized. All the movements should be slow, gentle, smooth and even, so that a sound foundation can be established. Only on this basis can the practitioner proceed to meet the requirments of flexibility, continuity, serenity and relaxation. Afterward, the practitioner can focus his attention on the transformation between emptiness and solidness, the regulation of breath, and the application of awareness.

It is also necessary to practice from a high stance to a low stance, to increase the momentum, especially for people in poor physical condition.

4) Persevere in practice.

Outwardly, it is not difficult to learn taijiquan, but one can grasp its extreme subtlety only if he studies with single-hearted devotion. The practitioner should not only study carefully, but must persevere in practice, so as to achieve the true essence of taijiquan and obtain its health-building and curative effects. If one works by fits and starts, as he goes fishing for three days and dries the nets for two, he will be unable to master taijiquan, and the beneficial effects will, as a matter of course, be out of the question.

6. Basic Training

Hands

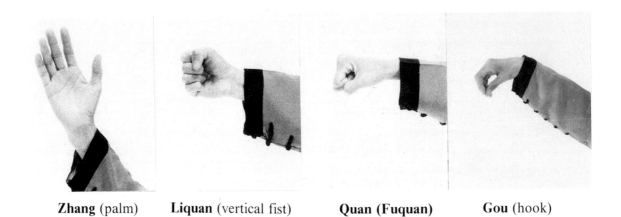

Zhang (palm)   **Liquan** (vertical fist)   **Quan (Fuquan)**   **Gou** (hook)

(fist or turn overed fist)

Stances

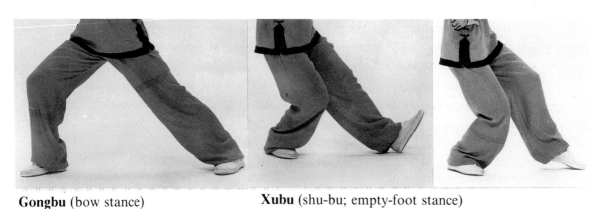

Gongbu (bow stance)   **Xubu** (shu-bu; empty-foot stance)

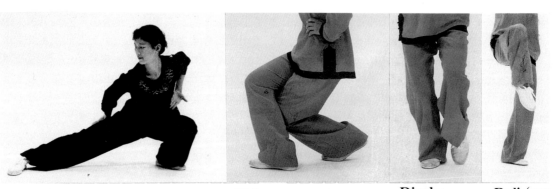

Pubu (dropping body stance)   **Xiebu**   **Dingbu**   **Duli** (one

(shie-bu; cross leg stance) (a letter "T" stance) leg stance)

7. Basic Movements

Step forward

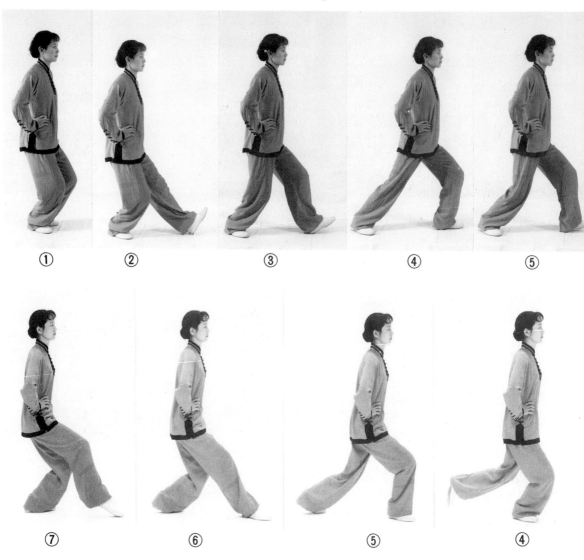

① ② ③ ④ ⑤

⑦ ⑥ ⑤ ④

24

⑥　　　　⑦　　　⑧　　　⑨　　　　⑩

③　　　②　　　①

Step backward

⑪　　　⑩　　　⑨　　　⑧

25

Yunshou (wave hands like clouds)

①   ②   ③

①   ②   ③   ④

④ ⑤ ⑥

⑦

⑤ ⑥

⑧

8. Simplified Twenty-Four Movements Taijiquan

1) The Names Of the Twenty-Four Movements

1. Opening Form
2. Part the Wild Horse's Mane — Left and Right
3. White Crane Spreads Wings
4. Brush Knee and Twist Step — Left and Right
5. Strum the Lute
6. Step Back and Roll Arms — Right and Left
7. Grasp the Bird's Tail — Left
8. Grasp the Bird's Tail — Right
9. Single Whip —Left
10. Wave Hands Like Clouds
11. Single Whip — Left
12. High Pat On Horse
13. Kick with Right Heel
14. Strike Ears With Fists
15. Turn and Kick With Left Heel
16. Descend and Stand On Single Leg — Left
17. Descend and Stand On Single Leg — Right
18. Work At Shuttles — Right and Left
19. Insert Needle To Sea Bottom
20. Flash the Back (Quick Defense and Push)
21. Turn, Deflect, Parry and Punch
22. Apparent Close-up
23. Cross Hands
24. Closing Form

2) Performance Of the Twenty-Four Movements

Movement 1
Opening Form

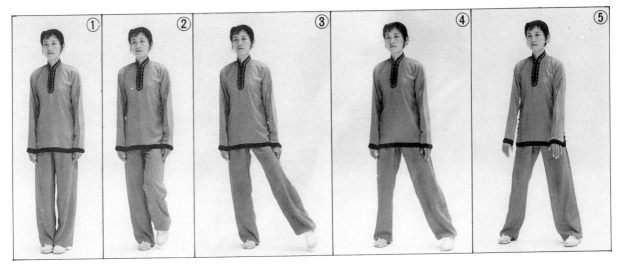

(1)
Stand upright with feet together, facing south, arms hanging down naturally. Be calm and keep the whole body relaxed. Look straight ahead.

(2)
Shift weight onto right leg. Then, lift left leg gently.

(3-4)
Left leg takes a step sideways, feet parallel to each other and about shoulder-width apart. Distribute weight evenly on both feet.

(5-7)
Raise arms naturally forward and upward to shoulder level with elbows slightly bent.

(8)
Bend knees and press palms down.

Movement 2
Part the Wild Horse's Mane — Left and Right

(9-10)
Turn torso slightly to the right and shift weight onto right leg.

29

(11-12)
Bring left foot next to right foot and rest toes on the floor. At the same time, right hand moves outward, upward and inward in a vertical curve until forearm comes in front of the right part of chest, while left hand moves downward and rightward until it comes under right hand. Both palms now face each other as though they were holding a large ball.

(13)
Left leg takes a step to the left, with the heel coming down first on the floor.

(14)
Turn torso to the left and shift weight forward. Meanwhile, separate arms gradually. Left arm moves obliquely forward and right arm obliquely downward.

(15-16)
As left leg bends at the knee, right leg straightens with its heel twisted rearward on the floor, toes pointing obliquely forward, to form a left "bow step". At the same time, raise left forearm forward and upward to shoulder level with palm facing obliquely upward. Right hand presses down simultaneously until it comes beside right hip, fingers pointing forward. Look at left hand.

(17-18)
Bend right leg slightly and shift weight backward.
Meanwhile, raise toes of left foot and turn them
outward before placing them on the floor again.

(19)
Shift weight forward, with toes of left foot pointing
outward.

(20)
Turn torso slightly to the left.

(21)
Draw right foot next to left foot and rest toes on the
floor. Meanwhile, right hand moves forward and
leftward until it comes under left arm. Both palms
turn over as though holding a ball in front of the
left part of chest.

(22)
As torso turns slightly to the right, right leg takes a
step to the right front with its heel coming down
first on the floor.

(23)
While weight is shifted forward gradually, separate
arms. Right arm moves obliquely forward and left
arm obliquely downward.

(24)
Repeat the movements in Figures 15-16, reversing
"right" and "left".

(25-26)
Shift weight backward while left leg bends slightly. Raise toes of right foot.

(27)
Turn toes of right foot outward before placing them on the floor again. As torso turns slightly to the right, shift weight forward onto right leg.

(28)
Draw left foot next to right foot and rest toes on the floor. Meanwhile, left arm moves forward and rightward until it comes under right arm. Both palms turn over gradually as though holding a ball in front of the right part of the chest.

(29-30)
As torso turns slightly to the left, left leg takes a step to the left front with its heel coming down first on the floor.

(31-32)
While weight is shifted forward, gradually separate arms. Left arm moves obliquely forward and right arm obliquely downward.

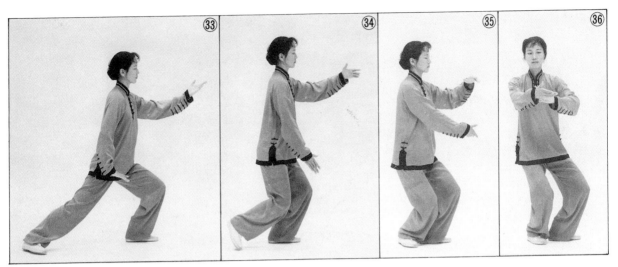

(33)
Repeat the movements in Figures 15-16.

Movement 3
White Crane Spreads Wings

(34-35)
Draw right foot a half step forward and place it behind the heel of left foot. Then, shift weight onto right leg. At the same time, right arm moves forward and upward with palm turned upward. Left palm turns downward simultaneously. Both hands now face each other, as though they were holding a large ball.

(36)
As torso turns a bit to the right, right hand moves upward and rightward, while left hand moves downward and leftward.

(37)
Look at right hand.

(38-39)
Turn torso slightly to the left. Move left foot a little farther with its toes gently resting on the floor to form a left "empty step". Meanwhile, right hand goes forward until it comes to the right front, with palm facing obliquely the right part of the forehead. Left hand presses down simultaneously until it stops beside left hip. Look straight ahead.

33

Movement 4
Brush Knee and Twist Step — Left and Right

(40-41)
Turn torso to the right and lower right hand. Left hand simultaneously rises up in a curve with palm turned upward.

(42)
Right hand continues to circle past abdomen to the right, while left hand goes rightward and then presses down with palm facing downward.

(43)
Bring left foot next to right foot and rest toes on the floor. Look in the direction of right hand.

(44)
Left foot moves a little farther toward the left front, with its heel coming down first on the floor.

(45-47)
Turn torso to the left and shift weight forward. As left leg bends at the knee, right leg straightens to form a left bow step. At the same time, right hand goes forward in a curve not higher than the head, elbow bent, and then continues to push forward to shoulder level. Left hand simultaneously presses down and brushes around left knee until it stops beside left hip. Leek straight ahead.

(48-50)
Shift weight backward and turn torso to the left with toes of left foot turned outward. Then, sift weight forward onto left leg again. At the same time, left hand comes backward and upward with palm turned upward, while right hand moves upward and leftward to the front of left shoulder with palm gradually turning downward.

(51)
Draw right foot next to left foot and rest toes on the floor. Look in the direction of left hand.

(52)
Right leg takes a step to the right front, with its heel coming down first on the floor.

(53)
While weight is shifted forward gradually, roll left arm and push left hand forwrd. Right hand simultaneously presses down and brushes around right knee.

(54)
Left leg straightens to form a right bow step. Left hand continues to push forward to shoulder level, while right hand comes beside right hip.

(55-56)
Shift weight backward and raise toes of right foot.

(57-59)
Turn torso to the right with toes of right foot turned outward. Shift weight onto right leg. Then, draw left foot next to right foot and rest toes on the floor. At the same time, right hand goes rightward and upward with palm turned up, while left hand moves across the face to the right and presses down.

(60-62)
Left leg takes a step to the left front with its heel coming down first on the floor. Then, turn torso to the left and shift weight forward to form a left bow step. At the same time, roll right arm and push right hand forward, while left hand brushes around left knee to the side of left hip.

Movement 5
Strum the Lute

(63)
Shift weight forward onto left leg.

(64)
Draw right foot a half step forward and place it behind left heel.

(65)
Shift weight onto right leg. In the meantime, raise left arm in a curve and move right arm slightly outward.

(66)
Left leg takes a step forward with its heel resting gently on the floor. Two arms move closer to each other, fingers pointing obliquely upward. Right hand now comes just beneath left elbow.

Movement 6
Step Back and Roll Arms
— Right and Left

(67-69)
Turn torso to the right and substitute toes of left foot for the heel on the floor. At the same time, right hand drops and then rises up in a semicircle to the right with both palms gradually turned upward. Look in the direction of right hand.

(70)
Turn torso to the left. Left leg takes a step backward with toes coming down first on the floor. Meanwhile, roll right arm and draw right hand forward.

(71)
While weight is shifted backward onto left leg, withdraw left hand. Right hand simultaneously pushes forward from above left hand.

(72)
Raise right heel slightly to form a right empty step. Right hand continues to push forward. Left hand comes to the side of left waist, palm facing upward.

(73)
Turn torso to the left. Left hand drops and moves backward in a semicircle.

(74)
Raise left hand to shoulder level, both palms turning up gradually.

(75)
Right leg takes a step backward with toes coming down first on the floor. At the same time, roll left arm and draw left hand forward.

(76)
Turn torso to the right and shift weight onto right leg. At the same time, withdraw right hand. Left hand pushes forward from above right hand simultaneously, both palms facing each other.

(77)
Raise left heel slightly to form a left empty step. Left hand continues to push ahead while right hand comes to the side of right waist.

(78-82)
Repeat the movements in Figures 68-72.

(83-86)
Repeat the movements in Figures 73-77.

Movement 7
Grasp the Bird's Tail — Left

(87)
Turn torso to the right. Meanwhile, right hand moves sideways up in a curve to shoulder level. Simultaneously, drop left hand.

(88)
Draw left foot next to right foot and rest toes on the floor. Both hands continue to circle to a position as though holding a large ball in front of the right part of chest, right hand on top.

(89-90)
Left leg takes a step sideways.

(91-92)
Turn torso to the left and shift weight forward. Bend left leg at the knee and straighten right leg naturally to form a left bow step. Meanwhile, move the rounded left arm forward with palm facing inward. At the same time, right hand presses down to the side of right hip with elbow slightly bent.

(93)
Extend right hand forward and upward until close to left wrist, with right palm turned upward and left palm downward.

(94-95)

Turn torso to the right and shift weight onto right leg. Meanwhile, pull both hands down in a curve and then to the right.

(96-98)

Raise hands to shoulder level. Then turn torso to the left and shift weight forward once again to form a left bow step. At the same time, ro!l right arm and place right hand inside left wrist. Both hands then continue to push ahead, with right palm facing forward and left palm backward.

(99)

Turn both palms down as right hand stretches forward from above left wrist.

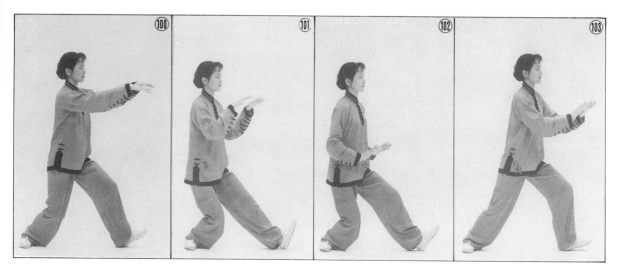

(100-102)
Separate hands slightly apart and shift weight backward onto the right leg which is bent slightly, with toes of left foot turned up. Meanwhile, draw both hands back and press them down in a curve until they come in front of the lower abdomen.

(103-105)
Slowly shift weight forward again to form a left bow step. Both hands simultaneously push forward and obliquely upward to shoulder level.

Movement 8
Grasp the Bird's Tail — Right

(106-107)
Turn torso to the right and shift weight onto right leg with toes of left foot turned inward. In the meantime, right hand makes a horizontal arc to the right.

(108-109)
Shift weight onto left leg. Bring right foot next to left foot and rest toes on the floor. At the same time, right hand moves downward and inward in a circle until it comes in front of the lower abdomen. Left hand goes to the front of chest. Both palms face each other as though holding a ball.

(110)
Right leg takes a step sideways.

(111-112)
Turn torso to the right and shift weight forward to form a right bow step. Meanwhile, push the rounded right arm forward with palm facing inward. Left hand simultaneously presses down until it comes beside left hip.

(113-114)
Extend left hand forward and upward until close to right wrist with left palm turned upward and right palm downward.

43

(115)
Shift weight backward and pull both hands down.

(116)
Turn torso to the left. Hands continue to move sideways with palms gradually turning upward.

(117-119)
Raise hands to shoulder level. Then, turn torso to the right and shift weight forward again to form a right bow step. At the same time, roll left arm and place left hand inside right wrist. Both hands then continue to push ahead.

(120)
Turn both palms down as left hand stretches forward from above right wrist, and then separate hands slightly.

(121-122)
Shift weight backward onto the slightly bent left leg, turning up toes of right foot. Meanwhile, draw both hands back and press them down in a curve until they come in front of the lower abdomen.

(123-124)
Shift weight forward slowly. At the same time, push both hands forward and obliquely upward.

Movement 9
Single Whip — Left

(125-126)
Turn torso to the left and shift weight onto left leg, with toes of right foot turned inward. In the meantime, left hand makes a horizontal arc to the left, while right hand drops and moves in a semicircle past the lower abdomen.

(127-130)
Turn torso slightly to the right and shift weight onto right leg. Bring left foot next to right foot and rest toes on the floor. At the same time, right hand makes an arc upward and around to the right. Then bunch the fingertips and crook the wrist to form a "hooked hand". Simultaneously, left hand goes in a semicircle past abdomen until it comes in front of the right elbow.

(131)
Left leg takes a step sideways with its heel first coming down on the floor.

(132-135)
Turn torso to the left and shift weight forward to form a left bow step. Meanwhile, left hand pushes ahead with palm gradually turning forward.

Movement 10
Wave Hands Like Clouds

(136-138)
Toes of left foot turn inward. At the same time, open right hand and turn palm outward, while left hand moves in a semicircle past abdomen to the right.

(139)
Shift weight onto left leg.

(140-141)
Turn torso slightly to the left. Bring right foot parallel to left foot and about 10-20 cm. apart. At the same time, left hand makes a horizontal arc to the left with palm gradually turning outward. Right hand moves simultaneously in a semicircle past abdomen to the left.

47

(142-143)

Turn torso slightly to the right and shift weight onto right leg. Right hand continues to rise up and makes a horizontal arc to the right, palm gradually turning outward. Left hand simultaneously moves in a semicircle past abdomen to the right. Left leg then takes a step sideways.

(144-148)

Repeat the movements in Figures 139-143.

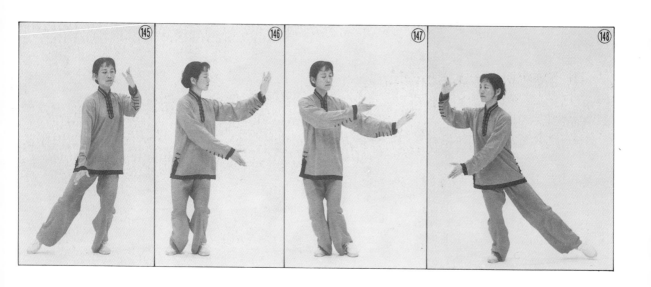

(149-153)
Repeat the movements in Figures 139-143.

Movement 11
Single Whip — Left

(154-155)
Turn torso slightly to the right and shift weight onto right leg. Meanwhile, raise left heel slightly and change right palm into a hooked hand. Left leg then takes a step sideways with its heel coming down first on the floor.

(156-158)
Repeat the movements in Figures 132-135.

Movement 12
High Pat On Horse

(159)

Draw right foot a half step forward and place it behind left heel. Open right hand and turn both palms upward while torso turns slightly to the right.

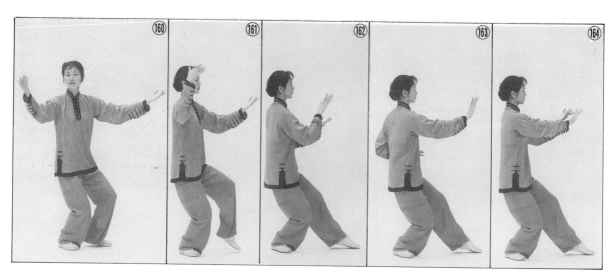

(160-163)

Shift weight backward onto right leg and turn torso to the left. Left leg moves a little farther with its toes gently resting on the floor, to form a left empty step. At the same time, withdraw left hand until it comes in front of the left hip. Simultaneously, roll right arm and push right hand forward from above left palm.

Movement 13
Kick With Right Heel

(164-165)

Raise left foot and step slightly forward. Meanwhile, cross hands by extending left hand forward and upward onto the back of right wrist, with left palm still facing upward. Two hands then separate, with palms turned obliquely downward.

50

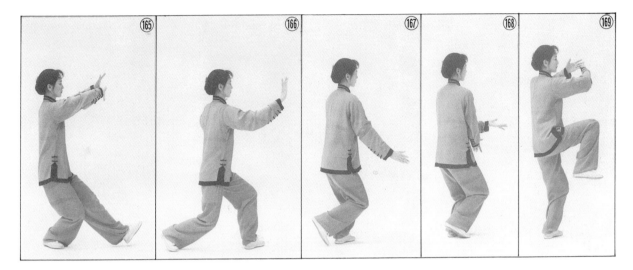

(166-168)
Shift weight forward onto left leg. Bring right foot next to left foot and rest toes on the floor. At the same time, both hands move in a circle, first outward, then downward and inward, until they cross in front of the chest, right arm on the outside.

(169-172)
Raise right leg with knee bent, and then straighten it slowly with its heel kicking towards the right front. At the same time, separate arms by extending hands to the sides at shoulder level with elbows slightly bent and palms turned outward.

Movement 14
Strike Ears With Fists

(173-174)
Bend right leg at the knee. Left hand moves next to right hand in front of the chest, with both palms slowly turning up. Both hands then drop in a curve past the sides of right knee.

(175-178)
Right foot drops slowly and takes a step to the right front with its heel touching the floor first. Then shift weight forward to form a right bow step. At the same time, both hands withdraw in an arc past waist, then outward and forward, palms gradually changed into loosely clenched fists. In the final position, with rounded arms, both fists move closer to each other at ear level, like pincers. The distance between fists is the same as the width of one's head.

Movement 15
Turn and Kick With Left Heel

(179-180)
Shift weight backward onto the slightly bent left leg and turn torso to the left, with toes of right foot turning inward. Simultaneously, open both fists and move left hand to the left side.

(181-183)
Shift weight onto right leg. Bring left foot next to right foot and rest toes on the floor. At the same time, both hands continue to circle, first outward, then downward and inward, until they cross in front of the chest, left arm on the outside.

52

(184-185)
Raise left leg with knee bent, then straighten it slowly with its heel kicking toward the left front. At the same time, separate arms by extending hands to the sides at shoulder level with elbows slightly bent and palms turned outward.

Movement 16
Descend and Stand On Single Leg — Left

(186-188)
Lower left foot by bending knee and place it to the side of right foot. Meanwhile, change right palm into a hooked hand with elbow slightly bent. At the

same time, left hand makes a horizontal arc to the front of right elbow.

(189)
Squat down on right leg. Stretch left leg sideways with toes turned slightly inward, keeping both soles close to the floor, to form a left "crouch step". Left hand simultaneously thrusts sideways along the inner side of left leg.

(190-192)
Turn toes of left foot slightly outward. Bend left leg at knee and straighten right leg as torso turns slightly to the left. Weight is thus shifted forward onto left leg. At the same time, left hand continues to extend forward while right hand drops behind.

(193-196)
Stand up slowly with left leg slightly bent. Meanwhile, bend right leg and raise it to waist level, keeping lower leg suspended. At the same time, open right hand and swing it forward past the outside of right thigh, then raise it with elbow bent, while left hand continues to rise and then presses down to the front of left hip.

Movement 17
Descend and Stand On Single Leg — Right

(197-198)
Lower right foot and place it in front of left foot. Then turn body to the left, using ball of left foot as a pivot. At the same time, raise left hand sideways to shoulder level and change it into a hooked hand, while right hand moves in an arc to the front of left elbow.

(199)
Squat down on left leg and stretch right leg sideways to form a right crouch step.

(200)
Right hand thrusts sideways along the inner side of right leg while moving down into the crouch step.

(201-202)
Turn torso slightly to the right and shift weight forward onto right leg. Right hand continues to extend forward and upward, while left hand drops behind.

(203-205)
Stand up slowly with right leg straight or slightly bent. Meanwhile, bend left leg and raise it to waist level, keeping lower leg suspended. At the same time, open left hand and swing it forward past the outside of left thigh, then raise it with elbow bent, while right hand continues to rise and then presses down to the front of right hip.

Movement 18
Work At Shuttles — Left and Right

(206-207)
Lower left foot and place it on the floor in front of right foot, toes pointing slightly outward.

(208)
Turn torso slightly to the left. Draw right foot next to left foot and rest toes on the floor. At the same time, move arms to a position as though holding a ball in front of the left part of chest, left arm on top.

(209-211)
Right leg takes a step to the right front as torso turns slightly to the right. Then, shift weight onto right leg to form a right bow step. At the same time, right hand moves upward until it pauses just above right temple with palm turned obliquely upward to form a defensive gesture. Left hand drops slightly and pushes simultaneously to the right front.

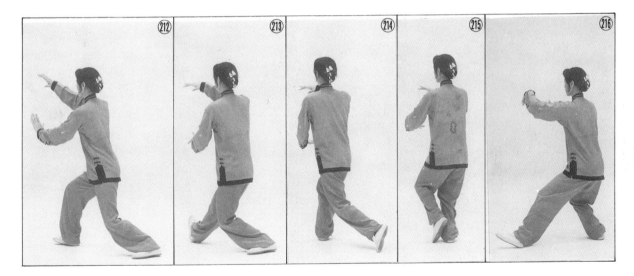

(212-215)
Shift weight backward, with toes of right foot slightly turning outward. Then turn torso slightly to the right and shift weight onto right leg again. Draw left foot next to right foot and rest toes on the floor. Meanwhile, lower right forearm to shoulder level, and move left hand slightly downward and rightward. Both palms face each other, right arm on top, as though holding a ball in front of the right part of chest.

(216-218)
Left leg takes a step to the left front as torso turns slightly to the left. Then, shift weight onto left leg to form a left bow step. At the same time, left hand moves upward until it pauses just above left temple with palm turned obliquely upward to form a protective gesture. Simultaneously, right hand drops slightly and pushes to the left front.

Movement 19
Insert Needle To Sea Bottom

(219-223)
Draw right foot a half step forward and place it behind left foot. Then, shift weight onto right leg as left foot moves a little farther, toes gently resting on the floor, to form a left empty step. At the same

time, turn torso slightly to the right. Lower right hand past right hip and move it sideways up to the side of right ear, elbow bent. As torso turns to the left, thrust right hand obliquely downward in front of the body. Simultaneously, left hand moves rightward, downward and then around to the side of left hip with palm facing downward.

Movement 20
Flash the Back (Quick Defense and Push)

(224-225)
Turn torso slightly to the right. Left leg steps a little bit farther forward, heel coming down first on the floor. Meanwhile, raise both arms, keeping left hand close to right wrist.

58

(226-227)
Shift weight forward to form a left bow step. At the same time, right hand continues to move upward, forming a defensive posture just above right temple, while left hand pushes forward at nose level.

Movement 21
Turn, Deflect, Parry and Punch

(228)
Turn torso to the right and shift weight onto right leg with toes of left foot turned inward. Right hand moves outward at the same time.

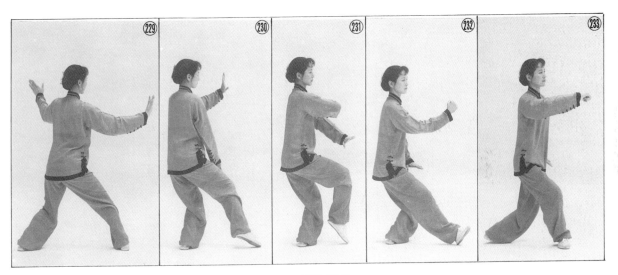

(229-230)
Shift weight onto left leg again. Bring right foot back in a small curve. At the same time, right hand circles rightward, then downward, while left hand moves upward and around to the right front of the body.

(231-232)
As torso continues to turn rightward, right leg takes a step forward with toes slightly turned outward. At the same time, right hand moves past abdomen with fingers clenched into a fist. Then, with forearm rotating outward and turning round, thrust right fist upward and obliquely forward to the right front, while left hand presses down to the side of left hip.

(233-235)
Shift weight forward onto right leg and step forward with left leg. Meanwhile, move left hand in a circular path outward and forward to the front of the body, and withdraw right fist sideways back to the side of right waist.

(236-237)
Shift weight forward to form a left bow step. Meanwhile, right fist thrusts forward, with left hand pulled back to the side of right elbow.

Movement 22
Apparent Close-up

(238)
Stretch left hand forward from below right wrist with left palm turned upward.

(239-240)
Bend right leg and shift weight backward slowly with toes of left foot turned up. Meanwhile, open right fist and separate hands slightly. Pull both hands back slowly to the front of chest with palms facing obliquely inward, then turn palms down.

60

(241-243)
Shift weight forward to form a left bow step. At the same time, both hands press down past abdomen and then push forward and upward to shoulder level.

Movement 23
Cross Hands

(244-246)
Shift weight onto the slightly bent right leg and turn torso to the right, with toes of left foot turned inward. Then turn toes of right foot slightly outward. At the same time, right hand moves in a horizontal arc to the right.

(247-249)
Shift weight slowly onto left leg, with toes of right foot turned slightly inward. Bring right foot a half step toward left foot, feet parallel to each other and about shoulder-width apart. At the same time, move both hands downward and inward.

(250)
Cross hands in front of abdomen. As legs are gradually straightened, raise the crossed hands to chest level, right hand outside and both palms facing inward.

Movement 24
Closing Form

(251)
Turn palms downward.

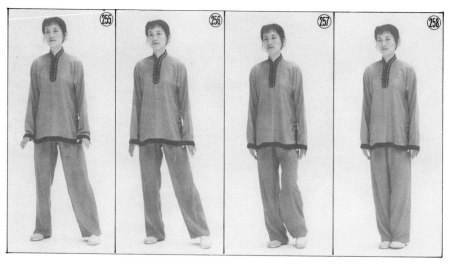

(252-255)
Separate arms about shoulder-width apart and lower both hands naturally to the sides of hips.

(256-258)
Shift weight onto right leg and bring left foot next to rihgt foot. Stand naturally. Look straight ahead.

9. Forty-Eight Movements Taijiquan

1) The Names of the Forty-Eight Movements

Opening Form
1. White Crane Spreads Wings
2. Brush Knee and Twist Step — Left
3. Single Whip — Left
4. Strum the Lute — Left
5. Pull and Push
6. Deflect, Parry and Punch — Left
7. Grasp the Bird's Tail — Left
8. Lean With the Trunk
9. Fist Under Elbow
10. Step Back and Roll Arms
11. Turn and Push With the Palm
12. Strum the Lute — Right
13. Brush Knee and Punch Down
14. White Snake Flicks Out Tongue
15. Slap Instep and Tame the Tiger
16. Throw Fist Diagonally Aside — Left
17. Fists Penetrate and Descend
18. Stand On Single Leg and Prop Palm Up
19. Single Whip — Right
20. Wave Hands Like Clouds — Right
21. Part the Wild Horse's Mane — Right and Left
22. High Pat On Horse
23. Kick With Right Heel
24. Strike Ears With Fists
25. Kick With Left Heel
26. Cover Hand and Wield Fist
27. Insert Needle To Sea Bottom
28. Flash the Back (Quick Defense and Push)
29. Separate Foot — Right and Left
30. Brush Knee and Twist Step
31. Step Forward, Catch and Strike
32. Apparent Close-up
33. Wave Hands Like Clouds — Left
34. Throw Fist Diagonally Aside — Right
35. Work At Shuttles — Left and Right
36. Step Back and Stretch Palm
37. Press Palms In Empty Step
38. Stand On Single Leg and Hold Palm Up

2) Performance of the Forty-Eight Movements

Opening Form

(1)
Stand upright with feet together. Keep the whole body relaxed. Look straight ahead.

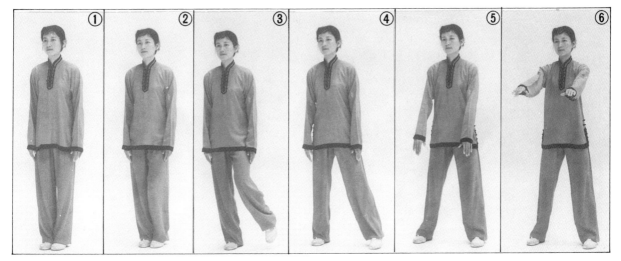

(2-3)
Shift weight onto right leg. Raise left leg naturally and then take a step sideways about shoulder-width apart, with toes pointing forward.

(4)
Distribute weight evenly on both feet.

(5-6)
Raise arms forward and upward slowly to shoulder level.

(7-8)
Bend knees and press palms down.

Movement 1
White Crane Spreads Wings

(10-11)
Shift weight onto left leg. Bring right foot next to left foot and rest toes on the floor. At the same time, right hand moves in a vertical circle rightward, downward and inward in front of lower abdomen, while left hand moves to the front of chest, both palms facing each other as though holding a large ball.

(12)
Right leg takes a step to the right rear.

(13-14)
Turn torso to the right and shift weight onto right leg. At the same time, separate arms. Right hand moves upward and rightward while left hand presses downward and leftward.

(15-17)
Turn torso to the left with toes of left foot resting on the floor to form a left empty step. At the same time, left hand presses around to the side of left hip, while right hand moves forward to the right front with elbow slightly bent and palm facing obliquely toward the right part of forehead.

Movement 2
Brush Knee and Twist Step — Left

(18-20)
As torso turns to the right (about 90 degrees), right hand moves forward and downward, then rises sideways up to the side of head with palm facing upward. Simultaneously, left hand moves upward and rightward, then presses down. Left leg then takes a step forward with the heel coming down first on the floor.

(21-23)
Turn torso to the left and shift weight forward onto left leg to form a left bow step. At the same time, roll right arm and push right hand forward to shoulder level, while left hand continues to brush around left knee until it comes to the side of left hip with palm facing downward.

Movement 3
Single Whip — Left

(24-25)
Shift weight onto right leg and turn torso slightly to the right, with toes of left foot slightly turned inward. At the same time, right hand makes a horizontal arc to the right.

(26-27)
Shift weight onto left leg and again turn torso slightly to the left. Bring right foot next to left foot and rest toes on the floor. At the same time, raise left hand in a curve until it comes to the front of chest, while right hand continues to circle downward and inward to the front of lower abdomen. Both palms face each other as though holding a ball.

(28-31)
Right leg takes a step sideways. As torso turns to the right, shift weight forward to form a right bow step. At the same time, both hands move forward in a horizontal circle with left hand adhering to right wrist, right palm facing obliquely upward and left palm obliquely downward.

(32-33)
Shift weight backward with toes of right foot turning inward. At the same time, right forearm continues to move rightward and backward.

(34-36)
Shift weight onto right leg. Bring left foot next to right foot and rest toes on the floor. Meanwhile, bunch fingertips of right hand and crook wrist to form a "hooked hand" at ear level.

(37)
Left leg takes a step sideways with its heel coming down first on the floor.

(38-40)
Turn torso to the left and shift weight forward to form a left bow step. Meanwhile, left hand pushes to the front with palm gradually turning obliquely forward. Look straight ahead in the direction of the left hand.

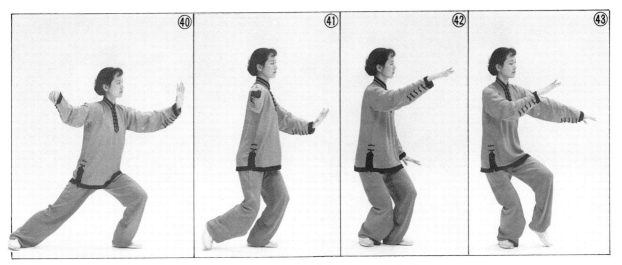

Movement 4
Strum the Lute — Left

(41-42)
Draw right foot a half step forward and place it behind left heel, then shift weight backward onto right leg. At the same time, open right hand and move it in a horizontal arc from side to the front. Drop left hand in the meantime.

(43-45)
Left leg takes a step forward with its heel gently resting on the floor to form a left empty step. At the same time, raise left arm in a vertical arc (slightly outward), and then move two arms inward until right hand comes just beneath left elbow.

Movement 5
Pull and Push

(46-48)
Turn torso slightly to the right and shift weight forward onto left leg to form a left bow step. At the same time, right hand stretches forward from above left palm. Both hands then move in a small arc to the right front, palms facing each other.

(49-51)
Turn torso slightly to the left. Draw right foot next to left foot and rest toes on the floor. Meanwhile, pull both hands down to the left in front of abdomen.

(52-54)
Right leg takes a step to the right front. Turn torso slightly to the right and shift weight slowly onto right leg to form a right bow step. At the same time, raise both hands to chest level and push them to the right front, keeping left hand adhered to right wrist, with right palm facing obliquely upward and left palm obliquely downward.

(55-57)
Turn torso slightly to the left and shift weight backward, turning up toes of right foot. At the same time, left hand stretches forward from above right palm. Both hands then move in a small arc to the left front.

(58-60)
Turn torso slightly to the right and shift weight onto right leg. Draw left foot next to right foot and rest toes on the floor. Meanwhile, pull both hands down to the right.

(61-64)
Left leg takes a step to the left front. Turn torso slightly to the left and shift weight slowly onto left leg to form a left bow step. At the same time, raise both hands to chest level and push them to the left front, keeping right hand adhered to left wrist with left palm facing obliquely upward and right palm obliquely downward.

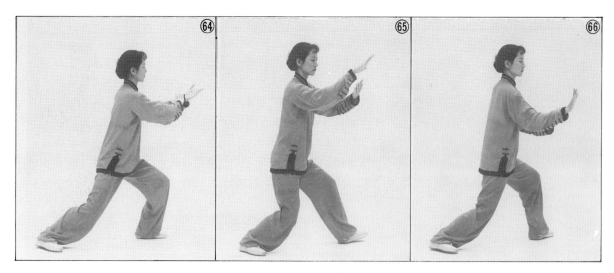

(65-75)
Shift weight backward, turning up toes of left foot.
Then, repeat the movements in Figures 47-58.

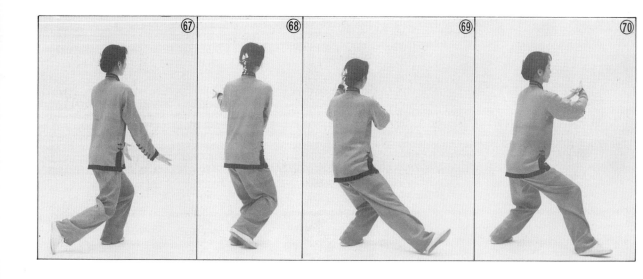

Movement 6
Deflect, Parry and Punch — Left

(76-77)

Turn torso slightly to the right and shift weight onto right leg. Draw left foot next to right foot and rest toes on the floor. At the same time, raise right arm sideways and bend elbow so that right hand circles to the front of chest with palm turned downward. Left hand simultaneously moves past abdomen with palm clenched into a fist.

(77-79)

As torso turns to the left, left leg takes a step forward with its heel coming down on the floor. At the same time, with forearm rotating outward and turning round, left fist rises and thrusts forward and leftward. Simultaneously, right hand presses down outside left arm until it comes to the side of right hip.

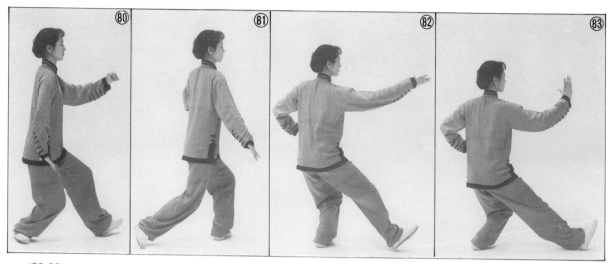

(80-83)

Shift weight forward onto left leg. Right leg then takes a step forward with its heel coming down on the floor. At the same time, right hand moves in a curve outward and then forward to the front of the body with fingers pointing upward. Meanwhile, withdraw left fist outward and backward to the side of left waist. Look forward.

(84-86)

Shift weight forward to form a right bow step. At the same time, left fist thrusts forward with arm slightly bent, while right hand moves back to the side of left elbow.

Movement 7
Grasp the Bird's Tail — Left

(87-88)
Shift weight backward with toes of right foot turned outward. Open left fist and lower right hand simultaneously.

(89-91)
Shift weight forward onto right leg as torso turns to the right. Draw left foot next to right foot and rest toes on the floor. At the same time, right hand circles sideways up until it comes to the front of chest, while left hand moves downward to the front of lower abdomen. Both palms face each other as though holding a ball.

(92-95)
Turn torso slightly to the left and step to the left front with left leg. Shift weight forward to form a left bow step. Meanwhile, move the rounded left arm forward with palm facing inward. Simultaneously, right hand presses down to the side of right hip, keeping elbow slightly bent.

(96)
Extend right hand forward and upward close to left wrist, with right palm turned upward and left palm downward.

(97-98)
Turn torso to the right and shift weight onto right leg. Meanwhile, pull both hands down in a curve and move them in front of right hip.

(99-102)
Raise hands to shoulder level. Then turn torso to the left and shift weight forward again to form a left bow step. At the same time, roll right arm and place right hand inside left wrist. Both hands then push ahead, with right palm facing obliquely forward and left palm inward.

(103)
Turn both palms down as right hand stretches forward from above left wrist.

(104-106)
Separate hands a little and shift weight backward onto the slightly bent right leg, turning up toes of left foot. Meanwhile, draw both hands back and press them down in a curve until they come to the front of the lower abdomen.

(107-109)
Shift weight forward slowly to form a left bow step. At the same time, both hands push forward and obliquely upward to shoulder level with elbows slightly bent and fingers pointing upward.

Movement 8
Lean With the Trunk

(110-111)
Shift weight onto right leg as torso turns to the right, with toes of left foot turning inward. Meanwhile, move right hand in a horizontal arc to the right.

(112-114)
Shift weight onto left leg again. Bring right foot next to left foot and rest toes on the floor. At the same time, move both hands downward and inward past abdomen and, with palms clenched into fists, cross hands in front of chest. Right arm is on the outside.

(115-119)
Right leg takes a step to the right rear. Turn torso to the right and shift weight onto right leg to form a right bow step. Meanwhile, separate fists, with arms slowly rotating inward. Right fist moves upward and rightward until it pauses in front of the right part of forehead, while left fist drops to the side of left hip, keeping both arms rounded.

Movement 9
Fist Under Elbow

(120-121)
Shift weight onto left leg and turn torso to the left, turning toes of right foot inward. Meanwhile, open right fist and move it leftward in a horizontal arc.

(122-124)
Shift weight onto right leg again. Bring left foot next to right foot and rest toes on the floor. At the same time, right hand comes to the front of chest, while left fist opens and moves to the front of lower abdomen with palms facing each other, as though holding a large ball.

(125-126)
Left leg takes a step to the left front with toes slightly turned outward. At the same time, move the rounded left arm forward and leftward while right hand presses down.

(127-129)
Turn torso slightly to the left and shift weight onto left leg. Draw right foot a half step forward and place it behind left heel. At the same time, left hand continues to circle with palm turned outward, then comes to the side of left waist with palm gradually turning upward. Right hand simultaneously moves in a curve past right waist, then outward and forward, with palm gradually turning upward.

(130-131)
Shift weight onto right leg. Left leg then takes a step forward with its heel resting on the floor. At the same time, left hand stretches forward, moving above right wrist and keeping arm slightly bent. Then, with forearm rotating slightly inward, sink left wrist so that left palm faces obliquely rightward with fingers pointing upward. Simultaneously, clench right palm into a fist and pull it back until it stops just beneath left elbow.

Movement 10
Step Back and Roll Arms

(132-134)
Turn torso to the right and substitute toes of left foot for the heel on the floor. Open right fist. At the same time, right hand drops and then rises sideways up to shoulder level. Turn both palms upward gradually. Look at right hand.

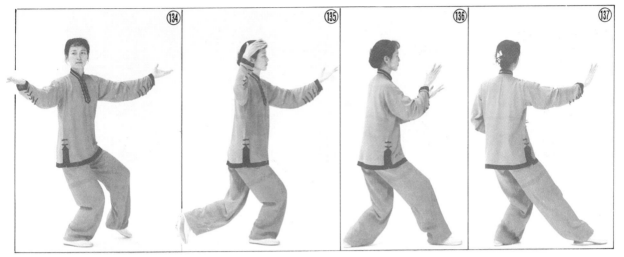

(135-137)
As torso turns to the left, left leg takes a step backward with its toes coming down first on the floor. As weight is slowly shifted onto left leg, raise right heel slightly to form a right empty step. At the same time, withdraw left hand to the side of left waist. Simultaneously, roll right arm and push right hand forward from above left hand, keeping wrist sunk, elbow slightly bent and fingers pointing obliquely upward in the final position.

(138)
Left hand drops and then rises sideways up to shoulder level. Turn both palms upward gradually. Look in the direction of left hand.

(139-141)
As torso turns to the right, right leg takes a step backward with its toes coming down first on the floor. As weight is slowly shifted onto right leg, raise left heel slightly to form a left empty step. At the same time, withdraw right hand to the side of right waist. Simultaneously, roll left arm and push left hand forward from above right hand, keeping wrist sunk, elbow slightly bent and fingers pointing obliquely upward in the final position.

81

(142)
Right hand drops and then rises sideways up to shoulder level. Turn palms upward gradually. Look in the direction of right hand.

(143-149)
Repeat the movements in Figures 134-141.

Movement 11
Turn and Push With the Palm

(150-152)
Left leg takes a step backward.

(153)
Turn torso leftward, using right heel and ball of left foot as pivots. At the same time, roll right arm, while left hand moves rightward and presses down, palm facing downward.

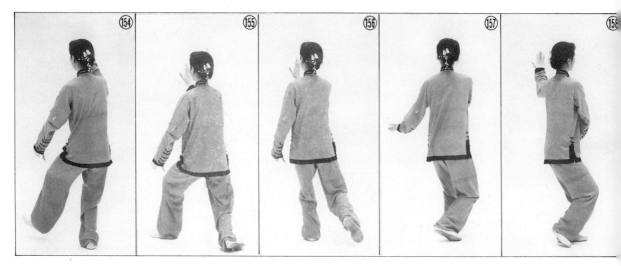

(154-156)

Left leg takes a step toward left front. Then, shift weight forward onto left leg. Draw right foot a half step forward, the ball of the foot resting behind the left heel. At the same time, right hand pushes ahead, keeping wrist sunk and palm facing forward in the final position, while left hand brushes around to the side of left hip with palm facing downward.

(157-158)

Turn torso rightward, using left heel and ball of right foot as pivots. Meanwhile, raise left hand sideways up to shoulder level with palm turned upward and then roll the arm. Right hand simultaneously presses down.

(159-161)

Right-leg takes a step toward right front. Then, shift weight forward onto right leg. Draw left foot a half step forward so the ball is behind right heel. At the same time, left hand pushes ahead, keeping wrist sunk and palm facing forward in the final position, while right hand brushes around to the side of right hip with palm facing downward.

(162-163)

Turn torso to the left, using right heel and ball of left foot as pivots. Meanwhile, raise right hand sideways up to shoulder level with palm turned upward and then roll the arm. Left hand moves rightward and presses down at the same time.

84

(164-165)
Left leg takes a step toward left front. Then, shift weight forward onto left leg. Draw right foot a half step forward so ball of the foot is behind left heel. At the same time, right hand pushes ahead, keeping wrist sunk and palm facing forward in the final position, while left hand brushes around to the side of left hip.

(166-167)
Turn torso rightward, using left heel and ball of right foot as pivots. Meanwhile, raise left hand sideways up to shoulder level and then roll the arm. Right hand presses down simultaneously.

(168-171)
Right leg takes a step toward right front. Then shift weight forward onto right leg. Draw left foot a half step forward so its ball is behind right heel. At the same time, left hand pushes ahead, keeping wrist sunk and palm facing forward in the final position, while right hand brushes around to the side of right hip.

Movement 12
Strum the Lute — Right

(172-173)
Move left foot a half step to the left rear and turn torso slightly to the left. Meanwhile, left hand comes to the front of the left part of chest with palm facing obliquely downward, while right hand rises to nose level.

(174-175)
Shift weight onto the slightly bent left leg. As torso turns to the right, raise right leg slightly and place its heel a little farther away on the floor, with knee straight, to form a right empty step. Meanwhile, move arms inward until left hand comes beneath right elbow with wrists sunk, to form standing palms in front of the trunk, right palm facing leftward and left palm rightward.

Movement 13
Brush Knee and Punch Down

(176-177)
Turn torso to the left with toes of right foot placed on the floor. Meanwhile, pull both hands down past lower abdomen to the left.

(178-180)
Turn torso to the right and shift weight forward onto right leg. At the same time, raise both hands to shoulder level, right palm facing upward and left palm downward. Both hands then move forward and rightward in a horizontal circle, keeping left hand close to right wrist.

(181-182)
Draw left foot forward and place it behind right heel. Shift weight onto left leg as torso turns to the left. At the same time, right hand continues to circle rightward and then across face to the front of left shoulder with palm gradually turning downward, while left hand drops and then rises sideways up to shoulder level with palm turning upward.

(183-186)
As torso turns to the right, right leg takes a step forward. While shifting weight forward to form a right bow step, roll left arm and then, with palm clenched, strike down with left fist from beside the left ear to the lower front beside right knee. Simultaneously, right hand presses down and brushes around right knee until it comes to the side of right hip.

Movement 14
White Snake Flicks Out Tongue

(187-189)
Shift weight backward and turn torso to the left, turning toes of right foot inward. At the same time, raise left fist and right hand, with fist facing downward and right palm upward.

(190-192)
Shift weight onto right leg and continue to turn leftward. Then, with toes of left foot turned slightly outward and heel of right foot raised, squat down slightly so that legs cross with left thigh resting on right thigh to form a left seated step. At the same time, open left fist and withdraw it to the side of left waist, with palm facing upward. Right hand pushes ahead simultaneously from above left hand with wrist sunk, arm slightly bent, and palm facing forward in the final position.

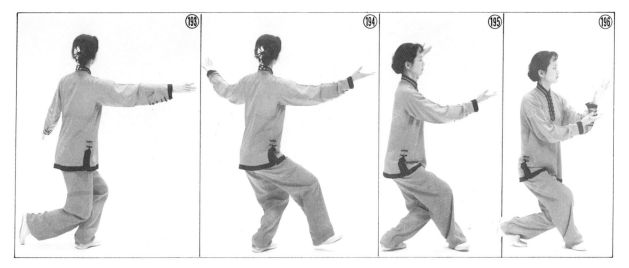

(193-194)
As the body rises slightly, right leg takes a step forward with toes slightly turned outward. Meanwhile, left hand moves rearward and then rises sideways up to shoulder level. Turn both palms upward simultaneously. Look at left hand.

(195-197)
Turn torso to the right and squat down to form a right seated step. At the same time, withdraw right hand to the side of right waist with palm turned upward. Simultaneously, roll left arm and push left hand ahead from above right hand. Look straight ahead.

Movement 15
Slap Instep and Tame the Tiger

(198-200)
Shift weight onto right leg and step forward with left leg. At the same time, right hand moves in a vertical arc rearward, upward and forward, to the side of the head, while left hand drops and then rises sideways up to shoulder level.

(201-202)
Shift weight onto left leg. Right leg then kicks to the upper front, keeping toes pointed. Meanwhile, right hand goes forward slapping instep of right foot at shoulder level.

(203)
Lower right leg, bending knee at the same time.

(204)
Place right foot across left foot on the floor. Both hands move in a horizontal arc to the right.

(205)
Left leg takes a step sideways.

(206-209)
Turn torso slightly to the left and shift weight onto left leg to form a left bow step. At the same time, both hands move in a curve past abdomen to the left, with hands gradually clenched into fists. Left fist then moves to the left front of forehead, palm facing obliquely upward, while right fist goes to the front of chest, fist palm facing downward. Keep both arms rounded. Look to the right.

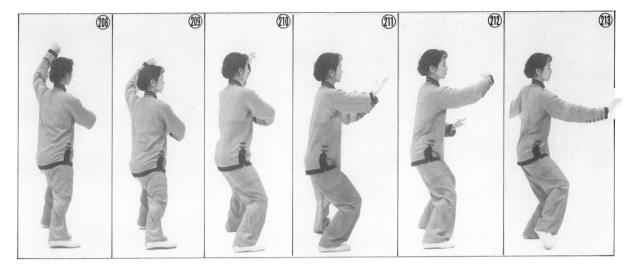

(210-211)
Shift weight backward and turn torso slightly to the right, with toes of left foot turned inward. At the same time, open fists. Left hand then drops to the front of chest, with palm turned upward.

(212-213)
Shift weight onto left leg. At the same time, right hand stretches forward from above left hand, palm facing downward. Simultaneously, left hand moves rearward and then rises sideways up to shoulder level.

(214-216)
Step forward and shift weight onto right leg. Left leg then kicks to the upper front, keeping toes pointed. At the same time, right hand drops and then rises sideways up to shoulder level while left hand goes forward, slapping instep of left foot at shoulder level.

(217-219)
Lower left leg, bending knee at the same time, and then place left foot across right foot on the floor. Simultaneously, both hands move in a horizontal arc to the left.

(220-224)
Right leg takes a step sideways (toward due right). Turn torso slightly to the right and shift weight onto right leg to form a right bow step. At the same time, both hands move in a curve past abdomen to the right, palms gradually clenching into fists. Right fist then moves to the right front of forehead while left fist goes to the front of chest, with both arms rounded. Look to the left.

Movement 16
Throw Fist Diagonally Aside — Left

(225)
Shift weight backward and turn torso slightly to the left, toes of right foot turning inward. Meanwhile, open fists. Right hand then drops to the front of chest, with palm turned upward.

(226-227)
Shift weight onto right leg. At the same time, left hand stretches forward from above right hand, then moves leftward with palm turned downward while right hand comes to the front of right hip.

(228-229)
Turn torso to the right. Bring left foot next to right foot and rest toes on the floor. At the same time, left hand drops past abdomen, palm clenched into a fist, while right hand moves in a vertical circle backward, sideways, and up, and then presses leftward.

(230-233)
As torso turns slightly to the left, left leg takes a step to the left front. Then, shift weight forward to form a left bow step. At the same time, raise left fist and, with forearm gradually rotating outward and turning round, throw it diagonally to the left front, keeping right hand adhered to left forearm. Fist palm faces obliquely upward in the final position.

Movement 17
Fists Penetrate and Descend

(234-237)
Shift weight backward, toes of left foot turned outward. Then, turn torso to the left and shift weight onto left leg again. Draw right foot next to left foot and rest toes on the floor. At the same time, with fist opened, left hand moves upward and makes a vertical circle sideways and down until it

comes to the front of lower abdomen, while right hand drops and then moves sideways up and inward to the front of the face. With both hands gradually clenching into fists and palms facing the trunk, cross arms in front of the body, left arm on the outside.

(238-242)

Squat down slowly on left leg and stretch right leg sideways to form a right crouch step. As torso turns slightly to the right, shift weight forward to form a right bow step. At the same time, left fist extends upward and moves to the left rear, while right fist drops from inside left arm and then penetrates along the inner side of right leg to the front.

From another angle

Movement 18
Stand On Single Leg and Prop Palm Up

(243-249)
Shift weight onto right leg, then stand up slowly with right leg straight or slightly bent. Bend left leg at knee and raise it to waist level, letting lower leg hang naturally. At the same time, open fists. Left hand moves forward past waist and then, with palm facing the trunk, stretches upward from inside right arm until it pauses just above and in front of forehead, palm gradually turning obliquely upward. Meanwhile, right hand moves up to nose level and then presses down to the front of right hip, palm gradually turning downward.

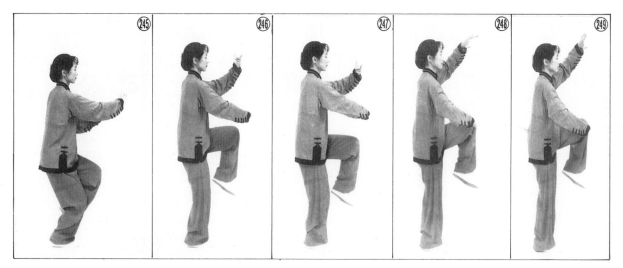

(250-253)

Step forward with left leg and shift weight onto left leg. Bend right leg at knee and raise it to waist level, letting lower leg hang naturally. At the same time, with palm facing the trunk, right hand stretches upward from inside left arm until it pauses just above and in front of forehead, palm gradually turning obliquely upward. Meanwhile, left hand presses down to the front of left hip, palm gradually turning downward.

Movement 19
Single Whip — Right

(254-256)

Lower right foot and step back. At the same time, right hand drops with palm turned upward, while left hand stretches forward and upward from above right palm. Then as torso turns to the right, shift

weight onto right leg and pull both hands downward and rightward.

(257-259)

Turn torso to the left and shift weight onto left leg. At the same time, raise both hands to chest level and move them forward in a horizontal circle, keeping right hand adhered to left wrist, with left palm facing obliquely upward and right palm obliquely downward.

(260)

Shift weight slightly backward, with toes of left foot turning inward. Meanwhile, left hand continues to circle leftward and backward with palm facing upward, using the elbow as an axis of rotation.

(261)

Turn torso to the right and shift weight onto left leg. Bring right foot next to left foot and rest toes on the floor. At the same time, left hand moves leftward to form a hooked hand by bunching fingertips and crooking wrist. Right hand moves to the side of left elbow at the same time.

(262-264)
Right leg takes a step sideways with its heel coming down first on the floor. As torso turns to the right, shift weight forward to form a right bow step. Meanwhile, right hand pushes to the front with palm gradually turning obliquely forward. Look straight ahead in the direction of right hand.

Movement 20
Wave Hands Like Clouds — Right

(265-266)
Turn torso to the left and shift weight onto left leg with toes of right foot turning inward. In the meantime, open left hand and turn palm outward. Right hand drops simultaneously.

(267-270)
Right hand continues to move in a semicircle past abdomen to the left. Then shift weight onto right leg and turn torso slightly to the right. Bring left foot parallel to right foot and about 10-20 cm. apart. At the same time, right hand rises and makes a horizontal arc to the right with palm gradually turning outward. Left hand simultaneously moves in a semicircle past abdomen to the right.

98

(271-272)
Turn torso slightly to the left and shift weight onto left leg. Right leg then takes a step sideways. At the same time, left hand continues to rise and makes a horizontal arc to the left with palm gradually turning outward. Right hand simultaneously moves in a semicircle past abdomen to the left.

(273-277)
Repeat the movements in Figures 267-272.

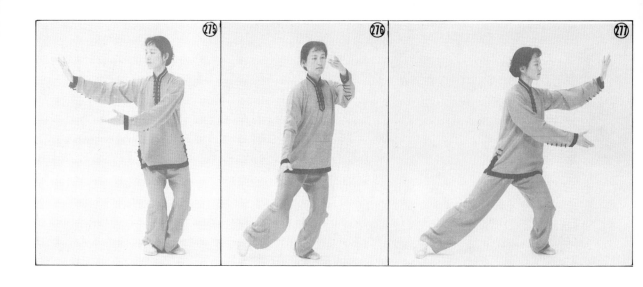

(278-280)
Repeat the movements in Figures 267-270.

Movement 21
Part the Wild Horse's Mane —
Right and Left

(281)
Shift weight onto left leg and raise right heel slightly. At the same time, right hand drops and moves to the front of lower abdomen, while left

hand moves leftward to the front of chest. Both palms face each other as though holding a ball.

(282-285)
As torso turns to the right, right leg takes a step to the right front. Then, shift weight forward to form a right bow step. At the same time, separate arms. Right hand moves forward and upward to shoulder level, with arm rounded and palm facing obliquely upward. Simultaneously, left hand presses down until it comes to the side of left hip, palm facing downward.

(286)
Shift weight backward onto the slightly bent left leg. Meanwhile, raise toes of right foot and turn them outward before placing them on the floor again.

(287-288)
Turn torso slightly to the right and shift weight forward onto right leg. Draw left foot next to right foot and rest toes on the floor. Meanwhile, left hand moves forward and rightward until it comes under right arm. Right hand simultaneously moves to the front of chest with arm bent. Both hands turn over so that palms face each other as though holding a ball.

101

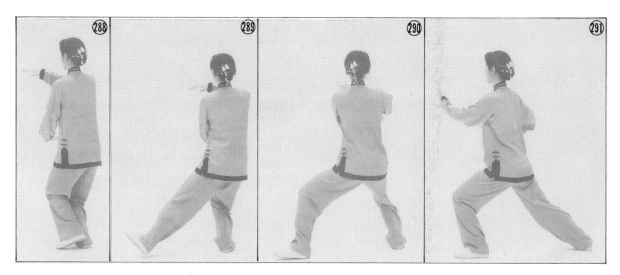

(289-292)

As torso turns slightly to the left, left leg takes a step to the left front. Then, shift weight forward to form a left bow step. At the same time, separate arms. Left hand moves forward and upward to shoulder level with arm rounded and palm facing obliquely upward. Simultaneously, right hand presses down until it comes to the side of right hip, palm facing downward.

Movement 22
High Pat On Horse

(293-295)

Draw right foot a half step forward and place it behind left heel. As torso turns slightly to the right, right hand rises sideways up to shoulder level with palm turned upward. Look in the direction of right hand.

(296-299)
Shift weight backward onto right leg and turn torso to the left. Left leg then moves a little farther forward with its toes gently resting on the floor to form a left empty step. At the same time, withdraw left hand until it comes to the front of left waist. Simultaneously, roll right arm and push right hand forward from above left palm.

Movement 23
Kick With Right Heel

(300-301)
Left leg steps to the left front. Then, shift weight forward onto left leg. At the same time, left hand makes a horizontal arc from side to the front and then withdraws slightly, while right hand moves rightward and backward past right waist, then stretches forward and upward from above left forearm.

(302-304)
Draw right foot next to left foot and rest toes on the floor. At the same time, left hand drops and then makes a vertical circle sideways up to the front of chest, while right hand continues to move in a vertical circle upward, rightward, and then downward and inward, so that both hands cross in front of the trunk with palms facing the body, right hand outside.

(305-306)
Raise right leg with knee bent, then straighten it slowly, kicking with right heel toward the right front. At the same time, separate arms by extending hands to the sides at shoulder level, with elbow slightly bent and palms turned outward.

Movement 24
Strike Ears With Fists

(307-309)
Bend right leg at knee and turn torso slightly to the right. Meanwhile, left hand moves next to right hand in front of chest, with both palms turned upward. Both hands then drop in a curve past the sides of right knee.

From another angle

(310-314)
Right foot drops slowly and takes a step to the right front with its heel touching the floor first. Then, shift weight forward to form a right bow step. At the same time, both hands move backward past waists, then outward and forward, palms gradually changed into loosely clenched fists. Both fists then move closer at ear level with arms rounded like pincers.

Movement 25
Kick With Left Heel

(315-316)
Shift weight slightly backward, with toes of right foot turning up. Meanwhile, open both fists and separate hands to the sides.

(317-319)
Shift weight forward onto right leg. Draw left foot next to right foot and rest toes on the floor. Meanwhile, both hands continue to circle downward, inward and upward, until they cross in front of chest, left hand outside.

From another angle

(320-322)
Raise left leg with knee bent, then straighten it slowly, kicking with the heel toward the left front. At the same time, separate arms by extending hands to the sides at shoulder level.

Movement 26
Cover Hand and Wield Fist

(323)
Turn torso slightly to the right. Lower left foot and place it next to right foot, toes resting on the floor. At the same time, both hands move to the front of the face, with right hand clenched into a fist.

(324-326)
Put right fist on left palm and lower them to the side of right waist with both palms facing upward. Left leg then takes a step to the left front. As torso turns to the left, shift weight forward to form a left bow step. At the same time, left hand moves around to the side of left waist with palm clenched into a fist. Simultaneously, thrust right fist forward with arm straightened and fist turned downward.

Movement 27
Insert Needle To Sea Bottom

(327-329)

Draw right foot a half step forward and place it behind left heel. Turn torso slightly to the right and shift weight onto right leg. At the same time, open both fists. Left hand then moves in a horizontal arc from side to the front and, following the body turn, presses rightward. Simultaneously, right hand drops and then rises sideways up to the side of head, arm bent.

(330-333)

Left foot moves a little farther forward with its toes gently resting on the floor to form a left empty step, while torso turns to the left. At the same time, thrust right hand obliquely downward in front of the body, fingertips leading the motion. Simultaneously, left hand presses down and brushes around to the side of left hip, with palm facing downward. Look to the lower front.

Movement 28
Flash the Back
(Quick Defense and Push)

(334-337)
As torso turns slightly to the right, left leg steps a little farther forward, with its heel coming down first on the floor. Then, shift weight forward to form a left bow step. At the same time, raise both arms to shoulder level, keeping left hand close to right wrist. Right hand then continues upward until it pauses just above right temple with arm bent and palm facing obliquely upward, while left hand pushes forward to nose level with wrist sunk in the final position. Look straight ahead.

From another angle

Movement 29
Separate Foot — Right and Left

(338-339)
Shift weight onto right leg and turn torso to the right with toes of left foot turning inward. Right hand simultaneously moves sideways.

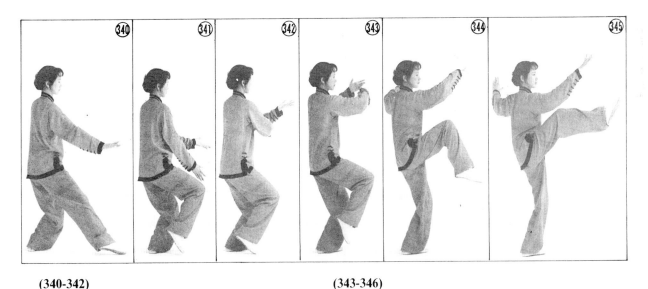

(340-342)
Shift weight onto left leg. Bring right foot next to left foot and rest toes on the floor. At the same time, both hands circle downward, inward and upward, until they cross in front of chest with palms facing the trunk, right hand outside.

(343-346)
Raise right leg with knee bent and straighten it with toes slowly kicking towards the right front, keeping toes pointed. At the same time, raise arms slightly and separate them by extending hands to the sides. Look at right hand.

(347-348)

As torso turns to the right, lower right foot and place it on the floor in front of left foot with toes turned outward. Meanwhile, left hand drops past left waist and then stretches forward and upward from above right arm.

(349-352)

Shift weight onto right leg. Draw left foot next to right foot and rest toes on the floor. At the same time, left hand continues to move upward, and then makes a complete vertical circle sideways and downward, while right hand drops past abdomen and then rises sideways up in a circular path, so that they cross in front of chest with palms facing the trunk, left hand outside.

(353-355)

Raise left leg with knee bent and straighten it with toes slowly kicking towards the left front, keeping toes pointed. Meanwhile, raise arms slightly and separate them by extending hands to the sides. Look at left hand.

Movement 30
Brush Knee and Twist Step

(356-357)
Lower left foot and place it next to right foot, toes resting on the floor. Meanwhile, move left hand in an arc to the front of right shoulder with palm gradually turning downward. Right palm simultaneously turns upward.

(358-361)
Left leg takes a step sideways. As torso slowly turns to the left, shift weight forward to form a left bow step. At the same time, roll right arm and push right hand to the front, palm facing forward. Simultaneously, left hand presses down and brushes around left knee to the side of left hip with palm facing downward. Look straight ahead.

(362)
Shift weight slightly backward, with toes of left foot turning outward.

(363-365)
Turn torso slightly to the left and shift weight onto left leg. Draw right foot next to left foot and rest toes on the floor. At the same time, right hand moves in an arc to the front of left shoulder with palm gradually turning downward, while left hand moves backward and then rises sideways, with palm turning upward. Look at left hand.

(366-369)
Right leg takes a step to the right front. As torso turns slightly to the right, shift weight forward to form a right bow step. At the same time, roll left arm and push left hand to the front with palm facing forward. Right hand simultaneously presses down and brushes around right knee to the side of right hip with palm facing downward. Look straight ahead.

114

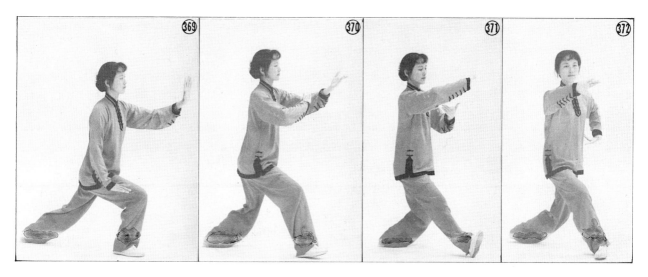

Movement 31
Step Forward, Catch and Strike

(370)
Shift weight backward, with toes of right foot turning outward. Meanwhile, stretch right hand forward and upward from above left hand, palms facing each other.

(371-374)
As torso turns slightly to the right, shift weight onto right leg and step forward with left leg. In the meantime, right hand makes a horizontal arc outward and backward to the side of right waist with palm clenched into a fist. Simultaneously, withdraw left hand past left waist and then move it from the side to the front with palm clenched into a fist.

(375-377)
Turn torso slightly to the left and shift weight forward by straightening right leg and twisting right heel rearward to form a left bow step. At the same time, right fist thrusts forward with fist facing leftward, while left fist withdraws until it comes under right wrist with fist palm facing downward. Look straight ahead.

Movement 32
Apparent Close-up

(378-379)
Draw right foot a half step forward and place it behind left heel. Meanwhile, open both fists and turn palms obliquely inward. Then, separate hands slightly.

(380-381)
Shift weight onto right leg and step forward with left leg. Meanwhile, withdraw both hands slowly to the front of chest, then press them down to the front of middle abdomen with palms gradually turning obliquely downward.

(382-383)
Shift weight forward to form a left bow step. At the same time, both hands continue to push forward and upward.

Movement 33
Wave Hands Like Clouds — Left

(384-386)

Shift weight onto right leg and turn torso to the right, with toes of left foot turned inward. At the same time, right hand makes a horizontal arc to the right with palm gradually turning outward. Simultaneously, left hand moves in a semicircle past abdomen to the right.

(387-389)

Shift weight onto left leg and turn torso to the left. Bring right foot parallel to left foot, about 10-20 cm. apart. At the same time, left hand continues to rise and makes a horizontal arc to the left with palm gradually turning outward. Simultaneously, right hand moves in a semicircle past lower abdomen to the left.

(390-392)

Turn torso to the right and shift weight onto right leg. Left leg then takes a step sideways. At the same time, right hand continues to rise and makes a horizontal arc to the right with palm gradually turning outward. Simultaneously, left hand moves in a semicircle past abdomen to the right.

(393-396)
Repeat the movements in Figures 387-389.

(397-400)
Repeat the movements in Figures 390-396.

Movement 34
Throw Fist Diagonally Aside
— Right

(401-402)
As torso turns to the left, left leg takes a step back to the left rear. At the same time, left hand moves in a small curve rightward until it comes under right

elbow with palm turned upward, while right hand stretches from above left hand towards right front with palm turned obliquely downward.

(403)
Shift weight backward onto left leg and pull both hands down to the left.

(404)
Turn torso to the left. Bring right foot next to left foot and rest toes on the floor. At the same time, move right hand past lower abdomen and clench it into a fist, with fist palm facing downward. Simultaneously, left hand goes in a vertical circle sideways and up, then presses rightward until it gets close to right forearm with palm facing downward. (See Figures 227-233).

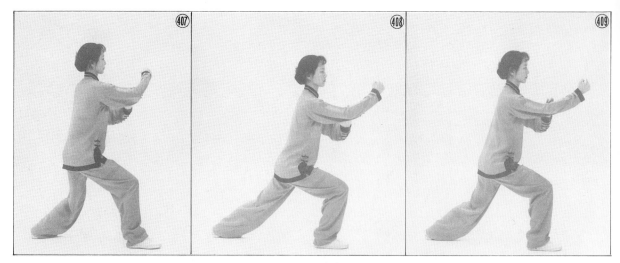

(405-408)
Right leg takes a step to the right front as torso turns slightly to the right. Shift weight forward to form a right bow step. At the same time, raise right fist and, with forearm gradually rotating outward and turning round, throw it diagonally to the right front, keeping left hand adhered to right forearm. Fist faces obliquely upward in the final position.

Movement 35
Work At Shuttles — Left and Right

(409-411)
Shift weight backward and turn torso slightly to the left. Meanwhile, open right fist and pull it slightly back as left hand stretches forward from above right hand. Both hands then move leftward in a small arc, with right hand coming under the inside

of left elbow, palms facing each other.

(412-414)
Shift weight forward onto right leg and turn torso to the right. Draw left foot next to right foot and rest toes on the floor. At the same time, pull both hands down from the left front past abdomen to the right, then raise them to shoulder level, with left palm facing upward and right palm downward.

120

(415-417)
Left leg takes a step to the left front. Turn torso to the left and shift weight forward. At the same time, both hands move in a horizontal circle forward and leftward, with right hand adhering to left wrist.

(418-420)
Draw right foot a half step forward and place it behind left heel. Meanwhile, left hand continues to circle leftward and backward, using elbow as an axis of rotation and keeping right hand adhered to left wrist.

(421)
Shift weight onto right leg and turn torso slightly to the right. Left leg then takes a step to the front. In the meantime, right hand moves to the front of chest, while left palm turns obliquely forward.

(422-423)
Turn torso to the left and shift weight forward to form a left bow step. At the same time, left hand moves upward until it pauses just above and in front of the left part of forehead, with palm facing obliquely upward. Simultaneously, right hand pushes to the front, with wrist sunk and palm facing forward in the final position.

121

(424-426)
Shift weight backward and turn torso slightly to the right. Meanwhile, lower left hand and turn palm upward. Simultaneously, right hand withdraws slightly, then stretches forward from above left forearm with palm facing downward. Both hands then move rightward in a small arc, with left hand coming under the inside of right elbow.

(427-428)
Shift weight forward onto left leg and turn torso to the left. Draw right foot next to left foot and rest toes on the floor. At the same time, pull both hands down from the right front, past lower abdomen to the left, then raise them to shoulder level, right palm facing upward and left palm downward.

(429-430)
Right leg takes a step to the right front. Turn torso to the right and shift weight forward. At the same time, both hands move in a horizontal circle forward and rightward, left hand adhering to right wrist.

(431-432)
Draw left leg a half step forward and place it behind right heel. Meanwhile, right hand continues to circle rightward and backward, using elbow as an axis of rotation and keeping left hand adhered to right wrist.

122

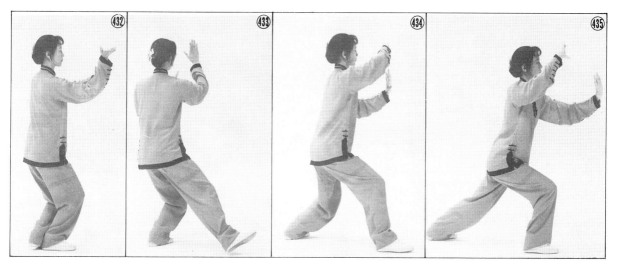

(433)

Shift weight onto left leg and turn torso slightly to the left. Right leg then takes a step to the right front. In the meantime, left hand moves to the front of chest while right palm turns obliquely forward.

(434-435)

Turn torso to the right and shift weight forward to form a right bow step. At the same time, right hand moves upward until it pauses just above and in front of the right part of forehead, palm facing obliquely upward. Simultaneously, left hand pushes to the front, with wrist sunk and palm facing forward in the final position.

Movement 36
Step Back and Stretch Palm

right hand drops to the front with palm facing obliquely upward.

(436-439)

Shift weight backward onto left leg and turn torso slightly to the left. At the same time, with palm first rotating outward, left hand moves in an arc leftward and backward to the side of left waist, palm gradually turning upward. Simultaneously,

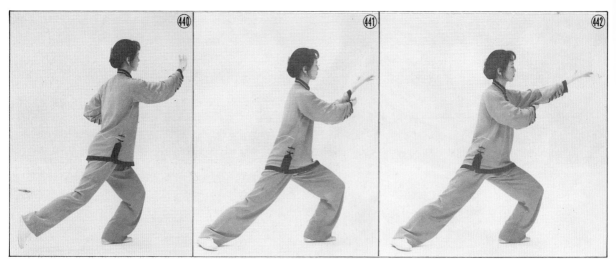

(440-442)

Turn torso slightly to the right. Bend left leg at knee and step back with right leg to form a left bow step. At the same time, right hand presses slightly leftward with arm bent and palm turned downward while left hand thrusts forward from above right forearm, with palm facing upward.

Movement 37
Press Palms In Empty Step

(443-445)

Shift weight backward onto right leg and turn torso rightward, with toes of left foot turning inward. Meanwhile, raise left hand by bending arm.

(446-448)

As torso continues to turn to the right, shift weight back onto the slightly bent left leg and move toes of right foot straight ahead to form a right empty step. Following the body turn, right hand presses down to the side of right hip with fingers pointing forward and palm facing downward, while left hand moves to the front and then presses down until it pauses just above right knee, fingers pointing rightward and palm facing downward.

Movement 38
Stand On Single Leg and Hold Palm Up

(449-451)

Stand up slowly with left leg straight or slightly bent. Bend right leg at knee and raise it to waist level, letting lower leg hang naturally. At the same

time, bring right hand up to chest level in front of the body, palm turned upward, while left hand moves to the left side at shoulder level with arm rounded and palm turned outward.

Movement 39
Shove With Forearm In Horse-riding Step

(452-456)

Lower right foot and place it on the floor in front of left foot, its toes turned outward. As torso turns slightly to the right, shift weight onto right leg and

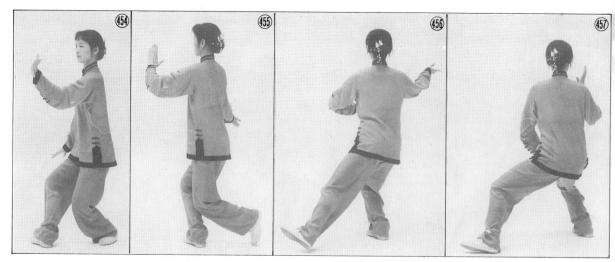

step to the left front with left leg. At the same time, right hand drops with palm turned downward and then rises sideways up to shoulder level with palm turned upward. Simultaneously, left hand moves in a horizontal arc around to the right with palm facing downward.

(457-459)
Shift weight slightly forward and turn torso slightly to the left to form a left half horse-riding step, keeping much of the weight on right leg. At the same time, lower left forearm past abdomen with palm clenched into a fist. Then, shove it forward above left knee, knuckles facing downward and fist palm facing obliquely forward. Simultaneously, move right hand leftward and put its palm on left forearm, helping the push with left arm. Look to

the left front.

Movement 40
Turn Round and Pull To the Full Extent

(460-462)
Shift weight slightly backward and turn torso

slightly to the right, with toes of left foot turned outward. Meanwhile, open left fist and move both hands slightly rightward, palms turned obliquely outward.

(463)
Shift weight forward onto left leg and begin to raise hands, with palms turned obliquely downward and fingers pointing to the right.

(464-465)
Right leg takes a step forward, toes turned inward, and about a foot's length from left foot. As body rises slowly, turn torso to the left and raise both arms forward to shoulder level.

(466)
As body continues to turn leftward, pull both hands around in a horizontal arc.

(467-468)
Left leg takes a step to the left rear, with right leg bent at knee, to form a right bow step. Meanwhile, pull both hands down, palms turned obliquely outward.

(469-470)
Shift weight onto left leg and turn torso slightly to the left to form a left crouch step. At the same time, clench palms into fists. As left fist withdraws to the

side of left waist, right fist presses down in front of the trunk, with arm bent at elbow. Both fist palms face upward in the final position.

Movement 41
Strike With Palm and Descend

(471-472)
Turn torso slightly to the right and shift weight onto right leg. At the same time, raise right arm until right fist comes to the front of forehead. Simultaneously, open left fist and stretch left hand from waist to the back of the trunk with palm facing rearward.

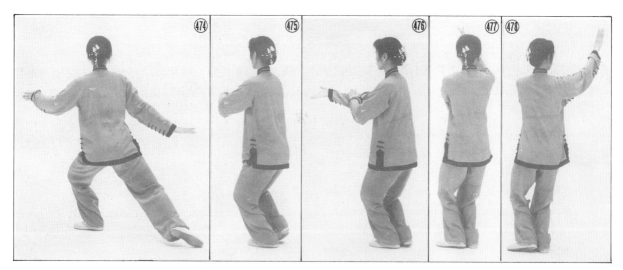

(473-475)
As torso turns to the left, turn toes of left foot outward and shift weight onto left leg. Draw right foot forward and place its ball behind left heel to form a T-step. Meanwhile, open right fist and lower it behind. Then, bring right hand forward past the outside of right thigh to the lower front, palm facing obliquely forward and fingers pointing obliquely downward. Simultaneously, left hands makes a complete vertical circle until it adheres to right forearm.

Movement 42
Step Forward and Cross Fists

(476-478)
Place sole of right foot on the floor and shift weight onto right leg. As torso turns slightly to the right, raise both hands and move them around to the right side. Left hand then pauses in front of right elbow, with palm facing inward.

128

(479-480)

Bunch fingertips of right hand and crook wrist to form a hooked hand. Then, squat down on right leg and stretch left leg sideways, with toes turned slightly inward, to form a left crouch step. Meanwhile, left hand drops to the front of crouch.

(481-483)

As torso turns to the left, turn toes of left foot slightly outward and shift weight onto left leg to form a left bow step. At the same time, left hand stretches forward along the inner side of left leg, then rises to shoulder level, while right hand drops behind.

(484-486)

Right leg takes a step forward, toes gently resting on the floor, to form a right empty step. Meanwhile, clench both hands into fists. As left fist withdraws slightly with its palm facing the trunk, swing right arm forward and upward with its palm facing obliquely forward, so that the two fists cross in front of chest, both arms rounded.

Movement 43
Stand On Single Leg and Mount the Tiger

(487-488)
Step back with right leg and open both fists. Turn torso slightly to the right and shift weight backward. At the same time, right hand drops and

then rises sideways up to shoulder level while left hand, following the body turn, moves in a horizontal arc to the right and then goes down.

(489-491)
Shift weight onto right leg to form a left empty step. As torso turns to the left, left hand moves past lower abdomen and rises to the left side at shoulder level while right hand rises and moves in a horizontal arc around to the left.

(492-496)
Turn torso slightly to the right and stand up slowly, with right leg straight or slightly bent. Meanwhile, raise left leg, keeping knee slightly bent and toes pointed. At the same time, right hand moves in a semicircle past the outside of left thigh to the front, with wrist sunk and palm facing forward in the final position. Simultaneously, bunch fingertips of left hand and crook wrist to make a hooked hand on the left side.

130

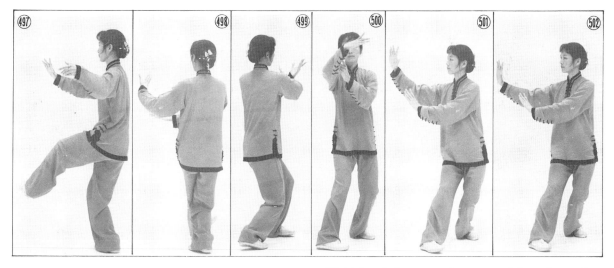

Movement 44
Turn Round and Swing Lotus

(497-499)
As torso turns to the right, lower left foot and place it across right foot on the floor with toes turned inward. Meanwhile, open left hand and, following the body turn, move it around in a horizontal arc.

Right hand then stretches upward from beneath left elbow. Both hands cross in front of chest with palms facing inward.

(500-502)
As body continues to turn rightward, both hands move around to the right side with palms turned outward.

131

(503-506)
Right leg swings toward the upper left and sweeps across face to the right in a fan-shaped arc, keeping knee straight and toes pointed. Meanwhile, both hands wave to the left, slapping instep of right foot successively in front of the face (left palm first, then right palm).

Movement 45
Bend Bow To Shoot the Tiger

(507-508)
As torso turns to the right, lower right leg and step to the right front. Meanwhile, both hands come down and move past abdomen to the right.

(509-511)
Shift weight forward to form a right bow step and clench both hands into fists. As torso turns slightly to the left, left fist thrusts to the left front at nose level with fist palm facing obliquely forward, while right fist moves up until it pauses in front of the right part of forehead with fist palm facing outward. Look at left fist.

Movement 46
Deflect, Parry and Punch — Right

(512-513)
Shift weight backward and turn torso to the left, toes of right foot turned inward. Meanwhile, open both fists and turn left palm up. Simultaneously, right hand stretches upward and rightward from above left hand, palm facing obliquely downward.

(514-515)
Bring right foot next to left foot and rest toes on the floor. At the same time, left hand drops, then makes a vertical circle sideways up to the front of chest, while right hand moves downward to the front of lower abdomen with palm clenched into a fist.

(516-517)
As torso turns to the right, right leg takes a step forward with its heel coming down on the floor. At the same time, right fist rises and, with forearm gradually rotating outward, thrusts forward and rightward. Left hand simultaneously presses down outside right arm until it comes to the side of left hip.

(518-520)
Shift weight forward onto right leg. Left leg then takes a step forward with its heel coming down on the floor. At the same time, left hand moves in an arc outward and then forward to the front of the body with fingers pointing upward. Meanwhile, withdraw right fist sideways back to right waist.

(521-522)
Shift weight forward to form a left bow step. At the same time, right fist thrusts forward, elbow slightly bent, while left hand moves back to the inside of right elbow, palm facing rightward.

Movement 47
Grasp the Bird's Tail — Right

(523-524)
Shift weight backward, toes of left foot turning outward. Open right fist and lower left hand simultaneously.

(525-526)
Shift weight forward onto left leg as torso turns to the left. Draw right foot next to left foot and rest toes on the floor. At the same time, left hand circles sideways and up until it comes to the front of chest, while right hand moves downward to the front of abdomen. Both palms face each other as though holding a ball.

(527-529)
Turn torso slightly to the right and step to the right front with right leg. Shift weight forward to form a right bow step. Meanwhile, move the rounded right arm forward, with palm facing inward. Simultaneously, left hand presses down to the side of left hip, keeping elbow slightly bent.

134

(530)
Extend left hand forward and upward until close to right wrist, with left palm turned upward and right palm downward.

(531-532)
Turn torso to the left and shift weight onto left leg. Meanwhile, pull both hands down in an arc and move them to the left.

(533-534)
Raise hands to shoulder level. Then turn torso to the right and shift weight forward again to form a right bow step. At the same time, roll left arm and place left hand inside right wrist. Both hands then push ahead, with left palm facing obliquely forward and right palm inward.

(535)
Turn both palms down as left hand moves forward from above right wrist.

(536-537)
Separate hands slightly and shift weight backward onto the slightly bent left leg, with toes of right foot turning up. Meanwhile, draw both hands back and press them down in a curve until they come to the front of lower abdomen.

135

(538-540)
Shift weight slowly forward to form a right bow step. At the same time, both hands push forward and obliquely upward to shoulder level, keeping elbows slightly bent and palms facing forward.

Movement 48
Cross Hands

(541-542)
Turn torso to the left and shift weight onto left leg, with toes of right foot turning inward and those of left foot outward. Meanwhile, left hand moves in a horizontal arc to the left.

(543-546)
Shift weight slowly onto right leg and bring left foot a half step toward right foot, with feet parallel to each other and about shoulder-width apart. At the same time, move both hands downward and inward until they cross in front of lower abdomen.

(547)
As legs are gradually straightened, raise the crossed hands to chest level with both palms facing the trunk.

Closing Form

(548-549)
Turn palms down and separate arms about shoulder-width apart.

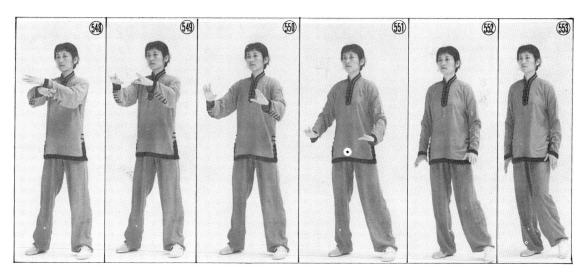

(550-552)
Lower both hands naturally to the sides of hips. Then, shift weight onto right leg.

(553-555)
Bring left foot next to right foot. Stand naturally, with toes pointing forward. Look straight ahead.

About the Technical Supervisor, Professor Wang Peikun

Address   : Room 508 4# Lane 542, Qing Yuan Huan Road, Shanghai, China
Date of Birth   : 4 July 1942
Education   : Department of Wushu, Shanghai Institute of Physical Education, Shanghai.(1960-1964)

Professional
  Background   : Instructor, Wushu Department, Shanghai Institute of Physical Education, 1965-1978.
                              Lecturer, Wushu Department, Shanghai Institute of P.E., 1979-1985.
                              Associate Professor, Wushu Department, Shanghai Institute of P.E., 1986— .
                              Deputy Dean, Shanghai Institute of P.E., 1984-1988.
                              Head of Wushu Department, Shanghai Institute of P.E., 1988—.

Professional Experience   : Captain, Wushu Team, Shanghai Institute of P.E., 1960-1964.
                              Head Coach, Wushu Team, Shanghai Institute of P.E., 1973—.
                              National-Grade Judge of Wushu, 1982—.
                              Member of Chinese Delegation and Chief Judge, Wushu Competition, Osaka, Japan, 1984.
                              Consultant, Shanghai Wushu Team, 1986—.
                              Member, China Wushu Science Academy Council, 1987—.
                              Member, Chinese Delegation and Chief Judge, First Asian Wushu Championship, Japan, 1987.
                              Consultant, Chinese Medical Rehabilitation Centre, U.S.A., 1987.
                              Guest lecture on Wushu, Japan Women's Sport College and the Association of Japanese Taiji Clubs in Tokyo, 1988.
                              Lecture on Wushu, Italy, National Wushu Association of Italy, 1989.
                              Deputy Chief-Judge for the International Wushu Invitational at the Wushu Festival, 1988.
                              Adviser, British Wushu Association, 1989.
                              Vice-Chairman, Shanghai Wushu Association, 1989.

Publications: : * The Study of Jumping Techniques in Wushu.
  (articles)   * Biomechanical Analysis of 360-degree Body Rotation With a Twist in Wushu.
                              * Continuation and Development of Changquan(Chang ch'uan)
                              * Analysis of "0" Type Legs In Wushu Plactitioners.
                              * The Possibilities of Wushu.
                              * The Characteristics and Exercise Methods of the Shaolin Thirteen Claws
                              * The Characteristics and the Exercise Methods of the Ground Techniques of Fukien.
                              * The Characteristics and the Exercise Methods of Staff Techniques
                              * The Question of Light Gongfu (Kung-fu)
                              * Nanquan (Nan ch'uan) Bridge Methods
                                (The above articles were published by the Journal of the Shanghai Institute of Physical Education)

(books)   :   * 100,000 QUESTIONS:
                                        Section on Wushu.
                             * WUSHU: One of the authors.
                             * SPORTS DICTIONARY:
                                        Section on Wushu.
                             * SHAOLIN THIRTEEN CLAWS:
                                        One of the authors.
                             * ZIXUEN CUDGEL:
                                        The author.
                             * FUJIAN DISHU: One of the authors.
                             * ZHOU MUO: The author.
                             * BROADSWORD PLAY:
                                        The author.
                             * CHINA CONCISE DICTIONARY OF WUSHU:
                                        One of the authors.
                             * THE DICTIONARY OF CHINESE MARTIAL ART:
                                        One of the authors.

ABOUT THE AUTHOR

Shing Yen-Ling was born in 1956, in Shantung Province, in the People's Republic of China. In 1977, she entered the Fukien Teachers' University and began training in taijiquan (t'ai-chi ch'uan); taiji (t'ai-chi) sword; whip and staff techniques; and other southern and northern style Chinese martial arts.

In 1980, she joined the physical education staff at the Fukien Medical College and began to teach Chinese martial arts to the students at the school. At this time, She also began studying baguazhang (pa-kua chang); shingyiquan (shing-i ch'uan); piguaquan (pi-kua ch'uan); liuge-daqian (liu-fu-da-chang; spear); fanziquan (fan-zhu ch'uan); and jiujie-bian (ju-jie bi'en; whip) in a special six-month seminar held at the Wuhan Institute of Physical Education, during which time she trained eight hours a day.

Ms. Shing moved to Tokyo, Japan, in 1988, where she began studying the Japanese language and teaching taijiquan. She was invited to the U.S.A. in 1989 by Mr. Higaonna Morio to perform a Chinese martial arts demonstration at the Miyagi Chojun Memorial Martial Arts Festival in San Diego, California. She will begin her study of physical education in the graduate school at Tokyo Gakugei University in April, 1990.

GLOSSARY OF CHINESE WORDS USED IN THE TEXT

(Pin-yin)	(Romanization)	(English Meaning)
Baguazhang	Pa-kua Chang	Eight-diagram palm
Changquan	Chang Ch'uan	Long shadow boxing
Chensue	Chen Sue	Chen style t'ai-chi ch'uan
Dishuquan	Diu-Shu Ch'uan	Foot techniques (on the ground)
Gongfu	Gong-Fu	Martial arts
Gun	G'uen	Staff techniques
Jiujie Bien	Ju-Jie Bien	Nine-knots-whip techniques
Nan	Nan	South
Nanquan	Nan Ch'uan	Southern style martial arts. Fukien style boxing. Southern Shaolin boxing
Shaolin	Shaolin	Shaolin style boxing
Sunsue	Sun Sue	Sun style t'ai-chi ch'uan
Taiji	T'ai-Chi	Great polarity; the original differentiation or manifestation of primal chaos into duality, symbolized by "yin" (negative principle; dark; void) and "yang" (positive principle; light; form); a philosophical concept relating to the duality of all things, implying the identity of supposed opposites.
Taijiquan	T'ai-Chi Ch'uan	T'ai-chi boxing
Taijijian	T'ai-Chi Jien	T'ai-chi Swordplay
Wusue	Wu Sue	Wu style t'ai-chi ch'uan
Wushu	Wushu	Martial arts
Yangsue	Yang Sue	Yang style Tai-chi ch'uan